Skipping through
the Pages
of Life

Skipping through the Pages of Life

by Peggy Hight Viverette

Copyright 2019

What you see,

write in a book…..

Revelation 1:11

This book is dedicated to God, Who gave me the gift of writing,

To my family for their love and encouragement,

To Steve Crain, for his inspiration and nudgings,

To Jonathan Scott, without whose assistance, this book would not be possible,

To Kristen and McKenzie for the cover of the book.

My Stories, My Babies

One of my favorite movie lines is from Gone With The Wind, when Prissy says "I don't know nothin' 'bout birthin' babies, Miss Scarlet!" It was with that attitude I began writing. I didn't feel that I had any gifting in that area or any area, to be honest. Since that time, I have realized that writing is a God-given gift that I am extremely grateful for. I compare writing stories to birthing babies now. My stories are my babies.

When I have an idea for a story, sometimes I see it as a picture, sometimes it will come from remembering something that has happened, or it might be a thought or an idea that seems to pop up in my head, like a trigger or prompt. It might be something that strikes me as funny or sad and the more I think about it, the stronger the urge to write it down becomes.

1

If it happens in the middle of the night, I have found, if I turn over and go back to sleep, it's gone – and becomes a miscarriage. With others I have written a note to remind myself to write the story later, but when I go back to my note, the idea is gone - the story was aborted. Each story that I lose saddens me. I grieve that I've lost what could have been.

Awhile back I lost part of my writings of two years or more when my computer crashed. I wasn't familiar with backing up material on my new laptop and by losing stories that couldn't be retrieved, I call this "the death of my stories."

I have learned some valuable lessons about my writings. Now, when I have what I call "an idea brewing," I try to go immediately to the computer, notebook or even a scrap of paper and start writing. Sometimes, the thoughts move so easily, the words start flowing and I can hardly write fast enough and before I know it, the baby is here. That's what I call an easy delivery.

Sometimes, though, it's hard to get the story going, every word is a struggle; seeming cold and lifeless. My brain is foggy, and my fingers don't want to move. That is a long, hard delivery. The labor was worth it, though, when, finally, another baby is birthed.

There are no cesarean births here. All my babies are birthed naturally. With each story, there is a period of labor involved, some being easy deliveries, others are harder, some intense. But each story, each of my babies is special and has a special place in a book that hopefully, the audience will love as much as I do.

My Favorite Things

Chocolate
Coffee brewing
Crawling under sheets that have been dried
in the sun
Gardenias
Rainbows
Rippling stream, cascading down the
mountain, bouncing off rocks
Freshly mown grass
Sunrise
Sunset
Gift of salvation
Field of grain, ready for harvest, rippling in
the wind
Eating the heart of a watermelon with my
hands
Miracle of birth
Picking greens, one leaf at a time
Music
God's love
Watching things grow
Tomato sandwiches

Walking on the beach
Meeting people
Gift of life
Being with family
Cards and letters that come just at the right time
Good friends
Hugs
Maddie
The smell and feel of a baby's skin
Laughter, especially belly laughs
Seeing a seed that has just popped out of the ground
Freshly ironed clothes
Joy that bubbles up from inside
Seeing people's lives turn around
Seeing old things restored, recycled, re-purposed
Seeing couples still together, holding hands after 50 + years of marriage
The promise of heaven
Writing stories
Watching clouds
The sound of rain
The freshness after a rain

Lilies

There, amongst the muck and mire blooms a
lily.
One in full bloom, another just beginning to
open.
There - another one, just a bud.
All at different stages, there amongst the
muck and mire.
Just waiting for the time to open up and
bloom,
there amongst the muck and mire.
So pure and white, untouched by the muck
and mire around it.
You lilies,
where are your roots?
There, amongst the muck and mire -
Yes, I see you.
You just sit there and float,
atop and amongst the muck and mire.

Lord, let me be like those lilies,
whether I'm a bud or in full bloom,
just waiting for my time to bloom.
Let my roots be in you,
just floating.

Help me to be, Lord, pure and white,
atop and amongst the muck and mire.

EARLY MORNING

In the stillness of early morning,
while watching the sun begin to break over
the awesome expanse of
the ocean...
the stillness wasn't even broken by a
passing seagull.
Even the dogs out for their morning walk
seemed to sense the sacredness of the
moment.

As I watched the sun struggling through
the panels of puffy clouds, climbing inch by
inch over the horizon,
I began to notice a change in the shells at
my feet:
all kinds of shapes and colors,
some with several different colors,
some broken,
some with barnacles attached to them,
some delicate,
others stiff and hard,
all having gone through the trauma of
damaging winds and waves.

Then something awesome began to
happen.
The colors of the shells began to change
from dull grays into the most beautiful
shades of pinks and lavenders
as the sun came into full view.
Those shells,
whether they were broken, unbroken,
fragile or strong,
dark or light,
became whole and beautiful in His light,
almost glowing in the sand around my feet.

So it is with us. No matter how much we've
been through, how the winds and waves of
life have battered and broken us, whether
we're fragile or strong, broken or whole,
walking with a limp or running a marathon,
when we allow His glorious light to shine in,
over us and through us, we become whole
and beautiful in His light, almost glowing to
those around us.

Life

In 1981, after a bout of cancer
God gave me a new lease on life

Like the prodigal son
I had wasted years of precious life
as I looked squarely in the face of death

Like a swimmer out in deep water
coming up for his last breath
I saw a raft to grab hold of

God gave me a second chance
I saw life as precious
I had to make the most of every day.
Every hour, every minute,
priceless.

The trees and grass
were greener.
Each day, new.

Family, friends,
my relationship with the Lord

treasures.

and
God's Word,
water to my soul.

I had found the lost coin.

The Heart Within

There's an old saying, "Don't judge a book
by its cover."

We don't see what's inside until it's opened
up

Neither can we see the heart within
God made us; all sizes, shapes, and colors
With different ideas, hopes and dreams
God made us all, just the way we are
And knows the heart within.

He loves us 'cause He made us
Had a good plan for us then
Has a good plan for us now
No matter who we think we've become
He never gives up on us
He sees who we can become
Just open up to Him
"Cause He knows the heart within.

Loneliness

Loneliness comes in like a cloud

Loneliness creeps in unawares

Loneliness comes in uninvited

Loneliness doesn't care if you're alone or in a crowd, but

Loneliness magnifies itself at night

Loneliness masquerades as mysterious, all the while,

Loneliness is an evil entity, seeking to pull you into its clutches

Loneliness wants you to think there's no hope

Loneliness is deceiving

Loneliness is defeated!

With God!

Evening

Sun dropping beyond the horizon
Unimaginable colors light up the sky
Darkness creeping in
Driving,
Watching lights popping on
An occasional plume of smoke
Drifting dreamily toward the sky
People sitting down for dinner
Laughing, talking, sharing
While others sit in
A cold empty house
With blinds closed
Lonely
Eating in silence
Others grab take out
After soccer, football practice, ballet
Dash in, eat on the run
Texting, tweeting
Facebook.
Chores and homework,
Collapse in bed,
While a galaxy of stars and moon fill the
night sky with beauty
Unnoticed.

The Darkest Hour

The darkest hour of my young
fourteen years,
was the day I came home from school,
expecting to find Mama there to greet me.
However, what I found was the house in
disarray,
a broken lamp
and pillows on the floor.
I was frantic,
with no telephone
and no one to ask
"what happened?
where is Mama?"

The first word I received was from
my sister,
who told me,
"Mama had a heart attack,
we'll finish the chores,
then I'll take you to see her"
No matter how much pleading I did,
she refused to take me to the hospital.

The next word was from my brother,
as I was bringing in the cows from the
pasture.
"Mama's gone", he said.
Finally he went on to explain,
"she's dead",
as Daddy sat silently in the car.

Dust on the Bible

There might be a little dust on the Bible if:

- You never pick it up.
- You think Jeremiah is the name of a pancake syrup (Aunt Jemima).
- You can't remember when you opened it up.
- When the Bible is only used for your family's genealogy.
- It's so heavy, you can use it for weight lifting.
- You think it's sacrilegious to set anything on top of it.
- You bought it from a traveling salesman, along with the encyclopedias.
- You pronounce Job as "job".
- You use it as a door stop.
- You've been known to literally <u>stand</u> on it.

The Rainbow

As a child, I was always fascinated with
rainbows and
used to imagine finding the pot of gold at
the end of it.
I would spend hours looking at the sky,
watching the clouds and
the changing of colors and shapes.
As I grew older, the fascination with the sky
and
God's amazing creation never dimmed.

Several years ago, while returning from
Toronto, Canada,
we stopped at Niagara Falls.
To my delight,
I saw one of the most spectacular sites I had
ever seen.
There, in the falls, were rainbows
everywhere
such beauty, such color.

I had found the pot of gold!

Insomnia

In the still of the night
whether I sleep or lie awake
I will praise you, Lord

When shadows are long
as the night drags on
I will praise you, Lord

When the old bones and joints
won't keep quiet
I say, praise the Lord, anyhow

As I lie awake and long for sleep
still - I will praise you, Lord

When the mind keeps rehearsing
the happenings of the day
I remind myself to
Praise the Lord!

As I anxiously await the dawn of a new day
I speak to my soul and say
Praise ye the Lord!

Then, when the sunlight streams through my
window
and tells my weary body to get up
I <u>will</u> praise the Lord!!

Bluebirds

What kind of heartless human being
would rip a bluebird house from it's post and
throw it,
along with it's nest of baby birds into the
highway
to be run over and crushed?
Surely you must have heard the little ones
crying
before you hurled them to their death.
I'm sure the parents did,
since they had stayed so close to their
babies,
taking care of them,
stuffing their hungry little beaks with
worms.

Perhaps you think no one noticed
as you committed this horrible act
in the shadows of darkness,
and that you "got away with it",
but remember, there is One who noticed,
One who saw the whole thing,
because He even knows "when a little
sparrow falls to the ground".

Spring's Fashion Parade

As I stroll around my yard, I notice that each
flower, each tree, each sprig of grass,
seem to be rejoicing that winter
is finally over and spring is here.
They all have shed their drab winter coats
and put on their finest,
beautiful colors of spring,
as if donning themselves for a fashion
parade,
each trying to outdo the other.
First came the pansies with their many
colored faces,
then came the daffodils,
bobbing their unique heads in the wind.
Then came the camellias,
forcing their beautiful blooms in spite of a
winter that almost killed them.
Then, bringing up the rear
of this fabulous parade are
the azaleas and dogwoods,
in all their glory
as if in preparation for Resurrection Day.
As to the winner of the fashion parade,
it's not over yet.

The Joys of Old Age

Nightly Routine:

! Vicks Vaporub for stuffy nose
! Chapstick for chapped lips
! Heating pad for arthritis
! Biofreze for aching knees
! Anti-fungus meds on toe
! Vaseline and white gloves for chapped hands
! Preparation H for hemorrhoids
! Sleeping pill
! Bandanna around my neck (just because)
! and don't forget to take those hearing aids and false teeth out....
! And we must not forget the many trips to the bathroom. It's no wonder I don't travel much anymore. With all this extra baggage I have to carry, it's just too much trouble!

Discarded Rose

A rose,
discarded,
seemingly without hope.
You pick it up, faded and wilted.
You give it hope.
Just a drink is all it needs,
Even after the petals are gone,
It can still take root and grow.

Not dead yet,
just wilted,
Just waiting for someone to notice.
You're there,
Just waiting.

Even if your petals are crushed,
You still give forth a fragrance that lives
on.

There's still hope,
Discarded rose.
Just trust and wait.

Blackbirds, Bluebirds and Painted Turtles

Blackbirds, bluebirds and painted turtles.
All sorts of what-nots.
Dust collectors are what I call them.
Where did all this stuff come from?
Was I starting some sort of collection or
were they souvenirs from another era.
How did I accumulate so many?
I envy those people whose houses are neat,
without those dust collectors sitting around.
But that's not my style.
Don't get me wrong, I'm not a hoarder but
my collectibles do require a lot of dusting.
They have sentimental value.
Each one has a story,
reminding me of the person who gave them
to me, or a memory stuck in my brain.
As each year goes by,
my collection grows,
as does the dust.
But they are my treasures,
so I'll just keep dusting.

Procrastination

Loved Ones Die

We Come

We Call

We Congregate

We Regret

We Forget

We Procrastinate

The Old Place

Washed out roads, exposed roots.

Beautiful old house; abandoned, roof
caving in,

Antique furniture, still there, just
waiting...

Old barn; padlocked.

Birdhouses on rotting posts;

stacked in a pile, waiting to be
refurbished.

Groves of dogwood and crepe myrtle
trees;

bare limbs exposed,

as if waiting to be dressed for spring.

Old toilet, car parts, bottles,

partially covered with leaves and pine
straw.

Sleepy old pond; snuggled among
massive trees;

Drainage pipe full;

waiting to be cleaned.

Will anyone return to save the old
place?

She's waiting…

When Love Went Away

You went away too soon,
I miss your voice, your ideas,
your hugs and kisses,
The sweet little unexpected gifts,
Big old, huggy bear,
and the little one we found on a walk,
the rides in the country,
the thunderstorms you loved,
I miss our talks, the plans we had,
holding hands, my head on your shoulder,
I miss your being here, your touch,
your scratchy mustache against my face,
The memories remain,
Still a void,
Longing to see you,
Someday, one day,
In heaven, with Jesus,
I'll hold your hand again.

Early Bird

"Early Bird" reminds me of the farm where I grew up. The farm included 600 acres, where we grew a number of crops, as well as cows, pigs, chickens, dogs, cats, sometimes horses, mules and other animals.

Mornings came early there, particularly in the winter, with so many animals to care for. The rooster was always the first one awake, with his cheery "cock a doodle do." Then the other animals would begin to wake up with their voices in symphony, all of them running to greet me, letting me know it was feeding time once again. I still remember the cold; chilling me to my bones, watching the steam from my mouth and theirs, as I leaned in to the warm bodies of the cows while I was milking. The cats were fascinating, as they drank their breakfast, still warm, straight from the "faucet."

As soon as the animals were fed and happy, it was time for me to run to the house, get cleaned up for a big healthy breakfast and ready to catch the school bus.

The Old "Hight" Farm

In 1941, we were forced to sell our farm in Hoffman, N.C., to the government. The U.S. Army wanted to build Camp Mackall.

My first childhood memory is from "the old place," as we called it. I was in the kitchen with Mama and saw her looking out of the windows as trees were being cut down. I noticed tears flowing down her cheeks, and I asked her why she was crying.

"They're taking our home away from us," she said.

We left that farm and moved to a house out in the country, as Daddy began searching for another farm. After about four years, Daddy finally bought a 600-acre farm in Aberdeen. He hired various carpenters and workers to renovate the house and build a barn and outbuildings. That beautiful piece of property soon became "home" as it took on the look of a stately plantation in my eyes. At the entrance of the property stood a large "pack house."

Open fields lay on each side of the driveway, and Daddy later planted apple trees along that driveway.

A large water tank, beside the pump house, towered over the farm. The huge barn held numerous stalls on one side, where the horses were housed. On the other side of the barn were stanchions with feeding troughs, which held hay for the cows to eat as they stood while being milked. We milked the cows usually by hand, but at one time we used milking machines when we supplied milk to a dairy.

Most of the flooring in the barn was made of concrete, which made it easier to clean. We kept feed for the animals in the center of the barn, as well as upstairs, where the grain was stored in huge bins and could be released for use downstairs. We also stored hay upstairs (in the loft) and could retrieve it through the double doors at the front of the barn.

A calf barn, with individual stalls, behind the barn was used to care for and wean calves from their mothers. A chicken house stood directly across from the barn. We used the front part of the chicken house for raising small chickens ("biddies," as we called them) and the back section was filled with nests for the laying hens. The upper part of the wall facing the barn was covered with mesh wire to provide ventilation in the "hen house."

In front of the main barn, a small cinder-block building was used for a dairy, where we brought the milk and placed it in milk cans for Montgomery Dairy to pick up.

Another building, closer to the house, served as a multi-purpose building. In the front part of that building was a spacious "washhouse," where a wringer washing machine and tubs, for rinsing the clothes, sat. Just outside stood the clotheslines and an area, just beside the building, where Mama rooted flowers. The room in the center of the building was used as a smokehouse, where we cured meat. At one time, before we started the dairy business, we kept a machine there that we called a "separator," which, when the milk was run through it, would separate the milk from the cream.

We used the back part of the building for storing wood and for raising "biddies" in the wintertime, when the baby chickens needed a light on them to keep them warm. The upstairs served as a fully equipped apartment, which was used by guests or workers, when needed. That building later burned.

The renovation of the house proved to be a major project. At the entrance of the backyard, Daddy had a rose arbor and cement walkway built that led to the steps. Upon entering the screened-in back porch, there were two entrances: one led into the kitchen, which held Mama's wood stove, as well as an electric stove. In the center of the kitchen, sat a huge, family-size, wooden table. At the end of the table stood what was called in those days a wooden "safe," with glass doors, where you could always find leftovers. The refrigerator was kept at the entrance of the large, walk-in pantry, which featured shelves on both sides stacked high with cans and jars of vegetables, meats, jellies, jams, and anything else needed for making a delicious meal. The other entrance on the porch opened into the hallway. To the left was a small bathroom with a claw-foot tub (we still kept an outdoor toilet, in case of emergencies). The next room on the left was a large, sunny bedroom. To the right stood the dining room, which later became the den; it had a big woodstove, and a big, comfortable chair, where Daddy liked to sit and smoke his pipe.

At the end of the hallway lay the living room, with another big woodstove which heated that part of the house. Daddy later replaced these stoves with oil heaters.

The living room had three doors that led into bedrooms and one door that led out to the front porch. A door to the left of the porch led to a "sun porch" or another bedroom. A fireplace was a special feature in the small bedroom to the right of the living room. That room became my bedroom when my sister left home.

Another special feature that Daddy had built was cement ledges and planter stands on each side of the steps. On these stands were large, matching planters, which usually held large ferns. Another cement walkway led out to the other rose arbor, identical to the one in the back yard.

On the farm, we grew corn, cotton, tobacco, peanuts and grains, as well as hogs, cows, and chickens for market. We also had a mule named Bob and a couple of horses. At one time on the farm, there was a little house (which later burned) and barn, which housed families who worked on the farm. On the rest of the property grew a forest of trees, many of them were beautiful pines, native to the area.

In the early 1960s, Daddy sold the farm to Peter Fleury and built a house nearby, where he lived until his death. Haskell and Gay Duncan later bought the farm. The old "Hight farm" – as I call it, in honor of my daddy, Urias Talmadge Hight – has since evolved into beautiful Camp Duncan, where young ladies are lovingly given a second chance at life. The camp staff helps mold and shape lives, giving young ladies a good foundation and helping them set goals for their lives and teaching them basic and Godly principles.

I am pleased and honored to see the transformation of our beloved farm into an even more beautiful place designed to help young women. I'm humbled to see the dedication, hard work, and faithfulness that have gone into making Camp Duncan a success, and I know that Daddy and Mama (who died when I was 14 years old), as well as Haskell and Gay, would be pleased also. I can just imagine them looking down from heaven, smiling.

The Kitchen

The kitchen on the farm had a sunny,
warm,
inviting "come on in and sit a spell"
kind of feel to it.
There was always room for one more at
the old farm table
and always something in the "pie safe,"
to munch on,
if nothing but a cold sweet potato.
In the summer time, a feast of fresh
vegetables, cornbread
and biscuits and maybe some "fatback" or
some other meat
that we had cured, was spread out for
family, field hands and
anyone else who showed up.
A cloth was spread over the leftovers to
save them for "suppertime."

In the wintertime, the old wood stove was
roaring,
filled with wood from the wood box,
behind the stove.

On the surface of the stove were all sorts
of pots and pans
filled with delicious-smelling food and,
of course,
cornbread and biscuits in
the "warmer" above.

The kitchen was always the gathering place
for folks who dropped by,
and there was always enough food,
no matter how many showed up.
Mama had a favorite saying when
unexpected guests arrived.
"Stay for supper," she'd say,
"I'll just scare something up."
And she always did.

Planting Peas

Everyone knows there are chores
to be taken care of when you live on a farm.
Some are daily chores, some weekly, some
occasional, and some are seasonal, such as
planting.

Planting was time consuming and always
boring to me, so the day Daddy sent me to
plant peas, I was not looking forward to it. It
was hot that day and I grew more bored with
every pea I planted. The routine was: dig a
hole, place three peas in the hole, and cover
up the hole; over and over again.

The job seemed endless. The end of each
row appeared to be miles away. I decided
there had to be a better way to finish
planting that bag of peas. Then, an idea
came to me. I was supposed to plant three
peas in each hole, but I thought, "What if I
put more peas in each hole? Who would
know?" So, I began pouring the peas in the
rest of the holes and I had used up all the
peas before I got to the end of that row.

After finishing the pea-planting chore, I decided to check for eggs in a nest that one of the stray hens had made in the "pack house." Before we moved to the farm, the pack house had been used for grading and packing peaches brought from nearby orchards. Since the peach trees were now gone, we used the pack house for storing equipment.

The hen that made her nest in the pack house liked to be different. She didn't want to lay her eggs near other hens in the chicken house. I think she thought that if she laid her eggs in a secluded place and no one found them, she could "set on them" and, before long, she would have a bunch of baby chicks and no one would know about them. It's in a hen's nature to do that.

But I had a plan, too: find the nest, take the eggs to the house, and place them in a pan of water. If the eggs didn't float, I would know they were still good and could be used or sold at the curb market.

When I arrived at the pack house, it seemed unusually dark inside, even though the sides of the pack house were not closed in. I waited a minute until my eyes adjusted to the dark; then I walked over to the hen's nest and reached my hand into the nest. The hen wasn't on the nest, so I felt around in the nest until my hand touched something icy cold. Suddenly, I knew what it was. It wasn't an egg – it was A SNAKE! I ran out of there as fast as I could.

As I ran, I became aware of a rattling noise, and I noticed that the faster I ran, the louder the rattling grew. I put "two and two together" and determined the rattling sound must be from the snake – a rattlesnake was chasing me!

I ran with all my might toward the house. Finally, exhausted, I fell on the ground and waited for the snake to bite me. I looked around. There was nothing behind me and the rattling had stopped. That's when I realized that the rattling sound came from the peas in my pocket – they were rattling!

A few weeks later, Daddy called me out to the field where I had planted the peas and showed me the result of what I had done. Even though I had forgotten about my "planting" and thought no one would know, the peas didn't forget. It was obvious I hadn't thought my plan through, because when the peas started coming up, much to my horror, huge mounds of peas were bursting out of the ground. That's when I knew I was in for one of Daddy's dreaded lectures, but by then, I had already learned my lesson.

My Daddy, My Hero

Though Daddy has been gone for many years, my memories of him are still vivid. I can still "see him" sitting in the den, on the farm, in front of the old stove, with one leg crossed over the other, smoking his pipe, deep in thought. When he had one eye closed, "citing his big toe", as we called it, you could believe "something was cooking." He was a farmer, a dreamer and an inventor. He came up with more inventions or ways to make a job easier, than we could keep up with. He was much older than my friend's dads, but he was a man I idolized. My brother and sisters used to say I had him wrapped around my little finger, especially when he would bring me little gifts. He came up with a game of "counting my ribs", while I sat on his lap. He had me convinced that I had a rib missing, telling me how important it was for me to be still so he could count them. Daddy had a dry wit and never smiled, so I would sit still as long as I could before I started wiggling and twisting; finally doubled over in laughter.

Though he never told me he loved me, I knew he did. He showed me.

After Mama died, I came to know a stricter dad and found his rules, sometimes harsh. Even though my friends were dating, Daddy stood by his rule that I couldn't date until I was eighteen years old, which, caused many "discussions."

Even though Daddy didn't go to church, (he faithfully drove me to church and picked me up every Sunday) observing the Sabbath was very important to him and there were certain things he didn't allow on Sunday. One Sunday, I sneaked into the pantry, set up the ironing board and was ironing my dress for church when Daddy walked in. He calmly told me to put the iron and ironing away and reminded me that I should have pressed my dress on Saturday and I would have to wear the dress as it was or find something else to wear. I also had to listen to his familiar lecture about cooking on Sunday, that "my mother planned ahead and cooked Sunday dinner on Saturday."

After I left home and got married, Daddy sold the farm and built a new house nearby. My sister and my nephew lived with him, as well as his beloved little Chihuahua, Chico. One of my favorite memories of him was seeing him drive up in his little black Ford Falcon very early on Saturday mornings, telling the children to get up, that "he had been up since before daylight!" The children's idea of Saturday mornings was to sleep late or watch cartoons. I think he enjoyed spending time with the grandchildren, but he always worried about them getting hurt. One particular morning, while he was sitting there on the couch, I remember him saying, "Peggy, make those younguns quit jumping off the roof, they're going to break a leg," to which I replied, "it's OK, Daddy, we've got insurance."

One of the children's favorite pastimes was, sitting around on the floor around Granddaddy's chair, listening to his, sometimes, scary stories. Kelly still remembers those special times when he took her to the library.

Daddy's later years were very difficult, as he went almost totally blind. He refused to let anyone take pictures of him; he didn't like for anyone to see him wearing the patch he had to wear over his eye.

About three weeks before he died, he had an accident. He was in the kitchen sometime in the wee hours of the morning, making coffee (this was his usual custom when he couldn't sleep). Whether he passed out before or after his pajamas caught fire, we don't know, but my nephew, Don, was asleep on the floor in the living room and heard him fall. Don ran into the kitchen and found him on the floor with his pajamas on fire. He was rushed to the hospital, where they performed surgery on his stomach. I remember Daddy begging us not to let them do the surgery. After the surgery, his blood type kept changing and they kept giving him transfusions. He never regained consciousness and it was finally determined that the cause of his death was an infection in his heart.

My daddy was a special man; he was my hero. Even though he only had a third grade education, he was brilliant.

Daddy used to try to help me with my homework and though he didn't know the formula to the math problems that the teachers wanted, he had a way of solving the problems and always came up with the right answers.

I have a copy of a patent of one of his inventions, which was shared with someone who stole it and made a fortune, according to Daddy. This invention is still being used today.

Mama's Unfinished Quilt

When I discovered Mama's unfinished quilt, I had all sorts of questions. Why didn't she finish it? Why did she sew the filling and the backing on it, without finishing the corner? As I examined the quilt more closely, I realized that the last row of quilting squares, somehow, was "off kilter" – they were not lined up as the other rows were. Maybe she became frustrated when she found her error and gave up on the quilt.

The more I looked at the quilt, the more I knew I had to finish it, so I took it to a quilter and asked her to finish it for me. When I returned to pick it up, much to my dismay, I saw that she had sewn in a solid piece of material that didn't match, rather than using material to match. Mama's quilt looked worse. So for years, I couldn't look at the quilt. I just left it folded up in a drawer.

How many times have we left projects and plans unfinished that left nagging feelings in the pit of our stomachs? Maybe we became frustrated when things didn't turn out as we expected and gave up our projects. Even in our walk with God, there may be dreams or even nudgings from God that we've put on the back burner, refusing to deal with them. It could even be sin in our lives, maybe unforgiveness, bitterness, hardheartedness and any number of things that we haven't dealt with. We know we need to do something about these things, but we procrastinate, like with the quilt, leaving them buried, folded up in a drawer. But then one day, we decide to do something about "that quilt," and we either pick up where we left off or begin over again. We can either leave it in that drawer, patch it up or cut out the bad material and put in fresh, new material.

I decided to take my quilt to my quilting instructor for advice. I was determined to finish it correctly but didn't know how to begin. The first thing that must be done, my instructor told me was to, "take out the old mismatched piece, then find something to match." After going through stacks of material, the near perfect match was found.

With a sigh of relief, I diligently began work on Mama's quilt. When I finished sewing in the new square, it looked as if it had been there all along and the questions I had in the beginning no longer mattered. Mama's Unfinished Quilt is no longer folded away in a drawer, but on display, finished, complete and beautiful, along with the other quilts that will be passed down to my children, along with my story of "Mama's Unfinished Quilt" story.

Learning to Drive

Patsy had been my best friend since we met in first grade at Aberdeen Elementary School. Even though I had lots of chores to do around the farm, she still liked to come home with me after school, spend the night, follow me around and watch me work. She also enjoyed riding around the farm with me, whether I was driving a car, a tractor and a truck. One day she decided she wanted me to teach her how to drive a car. When she continued to ask me, I finally agreed. As soon as she got in the driver's seat, I began to regret my decision. Growing up on a farm, I was driving before I could see over the steering wheel, so I carefully explained the ignition, the steering wheel, the gears, the clutch, the horn and the brakes, and how to use each one. I should have realized that she wasn't listening, as she kept saying, "I know, I know, let's go". When I felt fairly confident that she understood, I started the car and told her to put it in gear and slowly let the clutch out.

After several times releasing the clutch too fast, we finally chugged and jerked down the driveway, at which she thought was terribly funny. She continued to laugh hysterically as the car jumped and jerked along. We had started out in an open area between the pump house and the barn, then suddenly I realized that she had her foot on the gas and we were fast approaching the chicken house. As calmly as I could, I told her to take her foot off the gas and put one foot on the clutch and the other on the brakes. Instead of doing what I asked her to, she slammed her foot down on the gas. That's when I quickly placed my left foot on the brake, grabbed the steering wheel with both hands and turned it with all my might to the right. As the tires plowed into the ground in front of the chicken house and we came to a screeching stop, I was almost waiting for the impact. When I looked up and realized we hadn't crashed into the chicken house after all, I'm sure fire must have been streaming out of my nostrils as I screamed at my friend,

"DON'T EVER ASK ME TO TEACH YOU TO DRIVE AGAIN! YOU ALMOST WRECKED THE CAR, AND KILLED US BOTH."

With legs shaking, we got out of the car and checked for damage. The only trace of our harrowing experience was the ground that was plowed up in front of the chicken house. I dusted off the old Buick and carefully drove her back to the driveway. Supper time was especially quiet that night, as Patsy and I waited for Daddy to bring up the "car incident", but he didn't say a word, even though I'm sure he was enjoying watch us squirm. That was Daddy's way.

Hot Roast Beef Sandwich

One Sunday afternoon, the fellow I was dating asked me to accompany him to a pretty nice restaurant in town. I was thrilled at the thought of going to a real "sit down restaurant," since I'd never been to one. I was just a country girl, back in the '50s; we grew our own food and there were very few restaurants around.

As the waitress came to the table to take our order, I told Jack to order first, since I didn't know what to order. When he ordered a "hot roast beef sandwich," I said I'd have the same. So while we were waiting for our order, I began to imagine what it would look like. I was thinking, "okay, this should be easy, it's just a sandwich". Then, to my horror, when the waitress came out with that "hot roast beef sandwich," it was covered with gravy! I panicked. I imagined myself picking up that sandwich with my two hands and gravy dripping down my face as I attempted to eat it.

I guess Jack realized what was happening, as I continued to stare at it. What a relief to see him pick up his knife and fork and begin to cut it into bite size pieces!

Eatin' Watermelon

One of my favorite memories of growing
up on the farm was "eatin' watermelon."
Maybe that's why I still love eatin'
watermelon."
Nothing is quite as refreshing as taking
a watermelon break on a hot day.
The scorching days of summer remind me
of those long days working out in the
fields.
If a watermelon field happened to be
nearby,
I would find a small watermelon,
drop it on the ground,
reach down and grab
the juicy center of the watermelon, called
the "heart,"
sit down in the field
and eat until I couldn't hold another bite.

Wonder why watermelons don't taste quite
the same?
Was it the dirt, mixed with the juice
running down my face
that made it taste so good?

Or is it the memory of the "good ole days"
that is so sweet?

Aunt Hessie and Wanda

When I was growing up, Aunt Hessie was one of my favorite relatives. She was a jolly woman, seemed to always have a smile on her face and her home was a fun place to visit, in spite of the hardships which were a part of her life. Her husband, my mother's brother, died as a young man, before their youngest child was born. When Wanda was born, she was diagnosed with Down's Syndrome. She was a beautiful child, who proved to be a true blessing as she grew older. By that time, Aunt Hessie had become an invalid to crippling arthritis and Wanda was sent to a school where she learned to take care of, not only herself, but her mother and the household responsibilities, including learning to cook. Wanda rose to the occasion and was able to care for her mother and the house until Aunt Hessie died.

As long as Aunt Hessie lived, no matter what she was going through, she had a positive attitude, never complaining.

Even though she was bedridden and could only use one crippled hand, she used it to telephone people, to encourage them. And Wanda was always by her side, taking pride in the fact that she could handle the responsibility of taking care of her mother and the house. And she had the amazing ability to remember everyone's name and their birthdays, even the cousins.

Aunt Hessie and Wanda were always an inspiration and encouragement to me.

The Old Wood Shed

The old wood shed on the farm was a multi-purpose building. It not only was a wood shed, but it housed the laundry room (the wash house), which held the wringer washing machine and tin tubs for the rinse water and baskets for the clothes. Next to the wash house was the smoke house and creamery, where the meats were hung for curing, as well as where the milk was brought to from the barn and run through the milk separators (to separate the milk from the cream.) On the shelves around the room held jars of canned goods from the garden. The room on the back side of the building was where wood was stacked and from time to time I raised "biddies" (baby chickens) until they were old enough to be moved to the larger chicken house. Upstairs in the same building was an apartment (or extra bedroom when needed.) In the attic, extra household furniture was stored.

Outside, the front side of the building was where chickens were slaughtered for market. Soap was made in the old wash pot nearby. Alongside of the building, a cement walkway and ledge had been built. On the other side of the building, Mama had an area for rooting plants. On the same side of the building was the wire clothesline. A short distance from the clothesline was the second bathroom (the outhouse!)

This multi-purpose building was the scene of activity; a very busy place around the farm, that is, until the day of the fire. Evidently, the fire started from the wiring in the lamp which hung over the "biddies" and quickly spread throughout the building, becoming an inferno being fueled by the piles of wood. Since we didn't have a phone, by the time we saw the smoke and ran for help, the building was destroyed. All that was left besides charred metal and ashes was the cement foundation, walkway, ledge and lots of memories. The building was never rebuilt.

The Preacher

The preacher who stands out the most
in my memory
was my pastor as far back as I can remember
going to church.
He was the pastor/preacher I got saved
under; and speaking of "under,"
that is what stands out the most in my
memory about him.
I considered Preacher Caudle "old"
from the first time I met him.
I don't remember much about his preaching,
as I got saved in Sunday School,
but I do remember him baptizing me.
As he dunked me under (you know, the
Baptists believe in immersion baptism)
he forgot my name.
As he was holding me under, I was trying to
gurgle my name to him
and praying he would remember
before I drowned.
Finally, he remembered "Peggy!"
and I came sputtering up out of the water,
thankful I didn't die at the bottom of the
baptismal pool of the little Baptist Church
on Main Street in Aberdeen.

Tuna Sandwich and Hot Chocolate

I had a friend in the fifth grade who was perfect, or at least she seemed that way to me. Mary Ann had perfect clothes and her dresses were always neatly pressed. She even had galoshes to wear, to keep her shoes from getting wet when it rained. Her coat was green and blue plaid, was the same length as her dresses and even had a hood on it. When it was cold or rainy, all she had to do was pull it up over her head! Everything about her fascinated me.

I only remember Mary Ann being in my class for just that one year. It was the year the school burned and the classes had to be divided up and placed in different locations. The fourth and fifth grade combination was located in a building, which is now known as the AA building.

I guess what fascinated me the most about Mary Ann was her lunches. As I watched her pull her amazing lunches out of a beautiful lunchbox, I would sit and stare in amazement, especially on the days when she had a tuna sandwich, made with white, "loaf bread" neatly wrapped in waxed paper with a steamy thermos of hot chocolate! One day as I slowly pulled my ham biscuit out of a brown paper bag, she commented on how good it smelled, and without thinking, I replied, "do you want it?" To my astonishment, she asked me if I wanted to trade my "homemade" biscuit for her tuna sandwich <u>and</u> her hot chocolate! Again, without thinking, I said, "yes!" and within seconds I was savoring a lunch I had dreamed about. Mary Ann seemed to enjoy my ham biscuit as well.

The Work of a Farm

Growing up on a 600 acre farm, there was never a choice about work – it was expected and required. Taking care of the animals was the first priority and we always had cattle, pigs and chickens on the farm to care for. They all had to be fed at least twice a day and the baby calves and pigs were always hungry. Occasionally, a mother cow and pig would get sick, die or reject her babies and we would have to take over for the mother. Besides feeding and caring for the animals, the cows had to be brought into the barn and milked twice a day. We usually had four or five cows to milk and at one time we sold milk to Montgomery Dairy. During that time, we didn't milk by hand, but used a milking machine. We also made our own butter, which was one of my favorite chores.

Watching the butter come to the surface of the milk as I churned with a wooden paddle always fascinated me.

There was also the job of planting, caring for the crops, as well as the vegetable garden, harvesting of the crops, and canning or curing of the vegetables and meats.

"Early to bed, early to rise" was the motto of the farm and although life on the farm was hard, the work was rewarding and pleasant memories remain.

Our First Apartment

As newlyweds, we found our first little apartment in downtown Aberdeen. We were thrilled with it. It was actually rather cute; this little apartment, which was more like one room, divided up into a bedroom (a bed), kitchen (really?), very small sitting room, and a tiny bathroom. It had everything we needed, we thought – a bed, a stove (more like a half of a stove), a refrigerator (miniature), a sofa (for dwarfs) and a bathroom (more like a half bath, with a <u>folding door!)</u>.

We didn't mind the inconveniences, at first. After all, we were newlyweds! But one night, as I was cooking dinner on our little "half a stove", I heard a crash. I raced toward "other room", and found my 6'3" husband lying naked on the floor of our "very small sitting room". When I could finally catch my breath from laughing so hard, I asked him what had happened.

He told me he had slipped in the shower and fell through the folding door (and didn't see the humor of the picture). Thank God we weren't entertaining guests in the "very small sitting room" at the time.

Needless to say, we moved shortly after.

Moving, Moving, Moving

It didn't take long for Jack and I to outgrow our tiny little apartment on Main Street in Aberdeen.

Next, we moved into a little duplex apartment on Rush Street. The owner of the house, who lived in the other side of the house was a sweet, older lady who hovered over us like a mother hen.

When a two bedroom house on the same street became available, we jumped at the opportunity to move since I was pregnant with twins by then and we were needing more room. Lynne and Mark were born at the little brick house on Rush Street.

As it became more and more difficult to manage two babies, we moved out to the farm so that Daddy, and Ana, my sister, could help us with the babies. We stayed there for several months. I soon was pregnant with Kelly.

Our next move was to Pinebluff to a little one bedroom house. The living room became a nursery with two cribs. It was there that I was hospitalized six weeks before Kelly was born.

Before Kelly was born, we moved to a two bedroom house behind the school in Aberdeen. Lynne and Mark were 10 months old and crawling when Kelly was born (By the way, she had colic for six months.)

When Jack's mother was diagnosed with cancer, we moved to Asheboro so Jack could help care for her. Kelly was less than a year old; Lynne and Mark were toddlers. It was at that time I became very ill and was unable to properly care for the children.

So the children and I moved back to Aberdeen, to my brother U.T.'s log house, near the farm where Daddy and my sister lived. Jack stayed in Asheboro and came later. I was also pregnant with Jeff by that time. Lynne and Mark were three years old and Kelly was two when Jeff was born while living there.

Jeff was a baby when we moved to "the house under the hill," as we called it, a house that was used for farm workers. Daddy had a bathroom put in it, painted it and we lived there until Daddy had a house built for us.

After six years of moving, and 10 houses, we moved from the "little house under the hill." We finally had a permanent location, a new house; a home, where we moved to in 1963, where the children grew up and where I lived until I moved into town in 2017.

Sunday Picnics

From time to time on Sundays, on a beautiful, sunny day, after church, when the children were young, we would go on picnics.

Occasionally, I would get up early and fry chicken and make biscuits (there was no KFC back then) and <u>always</u> a jug of iced tea! This was our favorite menu, but if I hadn't prepared ahead of time and it was just one of those "lazy kind of days", a spur of the moment menu might just be peanut butter and jelly sandwiches. Everything always taste better on a picnic!

Sometimes we would pack up the car and drive to our favorite picnic spot, down in the woods, not far from the house. Other times, we would walk.

We would spread out blankets on the ground under the canopy of trees and sit around talking, laughing and savoring our meal and the beauty around us.

After we had stuffed our tummies, we would stretch out on the blankets, relax, listening to the sounds around us and watching the birds and squirrels chatting and playing in the trees. And maybe take a nap!

I miss those days.

The Big White Turkey

Have you ever followed one of those smelly turkey trucks with all those miserable creatures inside? I have to cover (partially) my eyes when I happen to be the car just behind one. But one particular day many years ago, when I was younger and more agile than I am these days, a big, white turkey fell off the turkey truck in front of my house. I couldn't believe my eyes when I saw him running down the highway, and all I could think about was "That poor turkey. After all he went through to survive his fall, he is going to be smashed by a car." So, I did what only seemed logical to me at the time, I dashed out the door and started chasing the big, white turkey.

I'm not sure whether I outran the turkey or he just gave up, but I'm sure of one thing: he had no idea how determined I was to catch him. I finally did grab him and walked home breathless with the big, white turkey in my arms.

Only when I closed the front door did I question what I had done and what I was going to do with the turkey. I called my husband and told him of my predicament, which, by the way, he thought incredibly funny. However, the butcher at the grocery store where my husband worked immediately came up with a solution. No matter how much I protested, against my better judgment, I finally gave in, and we had turkey for dinner that night.

The Games People Play

In our neighborhood, doors were left unlocked, neighbors knew each other, the kids played and had fun together. I always told my children that I wanted them "within hollering distance" so our house became the meeting place for the neighborhood kids.

There were always fun things to do in the neighborhood. There were 4 or 5 families who had children close to the same age who grew up together. Sometimes there were disagreements but they always settled them, one way or another.

Camping in our neighborhood meant grabbing all the sleeping bags and blankets they could find and dragging them out, along with snacks, (no tents) to the edge of the woods near the house and maybe, spending the night there.

Sometimes, it meant staying for the whole night; when they got rained out, that meant dragging those wet sleeping bags and blankets back home and sleeping on the living room floor. Or coming back home after a hitchhiker heard them laughing and talking and stopped by to join them. That gave them a good scare and they couldn't wait to get back home. These sleepovers, which almost always involved cousins and/or neighborhood kids, had to take place on weekends because no one got much sleep, including adults. And you had to be careful where you walked if you got up during the night – you might step on someone on a pallet on the living room floor.

Building was something else everyone seemed to enjoy. When they were very young, the girls liked to build playhouses and the boys built forts.

Later they joined forces and the fort became a clubhouse, then a bandstand and several other things according to how far their imaginations would take them.

Something that they didn't enjoy that much was gardening, but with a reward of going swimming after a day of getting hot and sweaty working in the garden, then being able to jump in the pond, they didn't mind so much.

Sunday afternoons were made for picnics, visiting and swimming in the pond. Swimming in my brother's pond on a hot day was everyone's favorite. Sometimes we would take sandwiches or snacks and have a picnic afterwards. Those were the "good, ole days", except for the time my brother forgot to tell us that the Pentecostals were coming down to the pond for a baptism and I had to come up out of the water and walk past a crowd of people in my skimpy bathing suit!!

Ballgames were another favorite activity. Everyone had a role to play, even me, as "Mama, the substitute pitcher," who always had bruised shins, for some reason.

Later on, all of "us kids" went through the motorcycle craze and there were always bicycles; therefore, bumps, bruises, cuts and scrapes. So, I was the designated neighborhood nurse. There were even a few times when I would have to transport someone to the ER for something more serious.

Besides being the neighborhood nurse, driver and substitute pitcher, I was den mother, counselor, and cook. Our multi purpose kitchen table served many purposes. There was always room for one more at the table. That table, which now resides at my new house, saw games played, counseling sessions, first aid performed, homework, crafts, building or repairing projects and any number of things that might come up. It was a gathering place for everyone to congregate, visit, chat and share.

What kinds of games do kids play today? Where do kids hang out today? What are they doing for fun? Who are their friends?

What kinds of games do adults play today? Who are our friends? What do we do for fun? Who are we hanging around?

What has happened to the family? Neighbors don't know each other like they used to. We don't visit like we used to.

What has happened to our country?

Playing with Fire

My son was always fascinated with fire. He liked to start fires, just to watch them burn. The higher the flames, the better he liked it. He especially enjoyed the fall of the year when we would rake up piles of leaves and burn them. On one occasion, the Fire Department had to be called, because, even with the help of all the children and neighborhood children, the fire was out of control. You would have thought the embarrassment of having to admit that he had started the fire would have diminished his enthusiasm for playing with fire, but it didn't.

One day, upon responding to the screams of his sister that he "was going to burn his brother at the stake", I arrived, just in time, to find my other son tied to a tree, sticks and leaves spread all around him and the "firebug" poised to light the match.

Another time, he set his pajamas on fire in front of his bed (thank God, he wasn't in them!). Luckily, I smelled smoke and was able to put the smoky mess out. He must have been disappointed that it was mostly smoke and no flames and gave up his career as an arsonist, later to become an optician.

Ode to the Old House on Laurinburg Road

Jeff was a baby when we moved to the tenant house on the farm where I grew up. Daddy had it painted and put a bathroom in at the back of the house. It was a cute little house that held many sweet memories. It only had one closet, which was between the bathroom and the back porch, where the wringer washing machine was kept (no dryer!) We heated the little house with a wood stove, and in the wintertime, the bathroom was very cold and the pipes that ran from the main house froze quite often, which meant no running water at times.

I recall one Christmas, I chopped down a little cedar tree in the woods behind the house, brought it in, put it in a bucket of sand and set it up in the living room. We thought the decorations we made for that little tree were gorgeous.

We lived there several years but as the children grew and Mark and Lynne started school, the little house became rather crowded.

In 1963, after a year of clearing land and building, Daddy presented my family with the keys to another little house (1166 square feet) he had built for our family. Mark and Lynne were six years old at the time; Kelly was five and Jeff was three. In spite of the fond memories of "the little house under the hill," we were thrilled to be moving from the tiny, four room tenant house into a brand new house – with its three bedrooms, and a warm bathroom. The house also had a carport and a storage room! When we moved in, the house seemed so big and the closets seemed enormous! We didn't have much furniture and with a picnic table in the kitchen we had plenty of room for all the kids, plus room for extras when needed. And we finally had a washer (no longer a wringer washing machine on the porch) and a dryer!!

The new house became a place for more sweet memories; fun times, the children growing up there, as well as good friends and neighbors.

The house, particularly the kitchen, became a hangout for the kids and their friends. There was always room for one more at the table and Mama's motto became mine, "stay within hollering distance" as they played, built playhouses, forts, stages, rode bicycles and motorcycles in the woods and fields around the house.

As the years went by, Jack and I went our separate ways, the children grew up, left home and the house felt big and empty again. For 54 years it had been home to the Clark/Viverettes. So, in January of 2017, I moved into town and the old house stayed empty for almost a year. Even though the house was still "home" it looked lonely and sad. It was time for a new chapter in its life.

On December 29,2017, the keys to "the old house on Laurinburg road" were turned over to its new owners. It now has a new family who is excited about "their" new home, making her their own and giving her a new lease on life.

Goodbye, "Old house on Laurinburg road," thanks for the memories!

The Lesson I Learned from a Four Year Old

I had not sought out the job of teaching this Bible school class of rambunctious 4 and 5 year olds, but due to a shortage of teachers I had agreed to teach the class even though I was recovering from surgery. The class was one big bundle of energy – full of giggles and high pitched noise, of which I never seemed to be able to raise my voice above and within minutes of standing before this class, I regretted my decision.

As rowdy as the class was, one little girl outdid herself. I don't remember her sitting in her chair, as she was told, for even a minute and every time I tried to talk, she talked. This went on for the entire lesson.

Finally, my patience was gone and I told her, "since you seem to know more about the lesson than I do, why don't you come up front and tell the class what you learned today?" So, she did. She stood up and repeated almost word for word the whole story, as I had told it!

Needless to say, I was in shock and I had to admit that I learned something that day from a little blonde haired four year old.

Memories of the Doctors

I went to work for the doctors, Dr. Morris and Tillie Caddell, a husband and wife team, in their little office in Aberdeen NC shortly after graduating from high school. It was my first real paying job and I thought $25.00 a week was big money, since working on the farm was a non paying job. I was hired as the receptionist, but I soon found out that working in a doctor's office was similar to farm work, in that, you never knew what you might be doing. Most of the time I was in the front area, greeting patients, taking care of the records and receiving payments, but if the nurse was busy, I might be assisting one of the doctors in an exam room or anything else that needed to be done. I met some of the most interesting people, many became friends. One of the most interesting patients was a man, who came in with a gunshot in his leg. In an attempt to obtain information and to take his mind off his pain, I asked him who shot him. He replied, "my friend."

Some days, I would pick up the mail at the post office or chocolate doughnuts from the grocery store. One day, Dr. Morris handed me the keys to his new car and told me to go pick up something for him. I took one look at that shiny new car, came back in and told him I couldn't drive that fancy car and handed the keys to him. However, when he wouldn't take no for an answer, I was soon screeching out of the driveway, fearing for my life and everyone I met. There were other days when the babysitter didn't show up, and I was nominated to be the babysitter. So, I would again take their car and their boys and head to their house for the day.

It was in that office that I met my husband to be; soon we were married and before long we were expecting. I continued to work and began to gain weight rapidly, so Dr. Morris was concerned and cut out my snacks. Every time he heard the refrigerator door, he would yell from wherever he was, even if he was with a patient, "Peggy, get out of the refrigerator." It was a difficult pregnancy, nausea and vomiting the whole time, so I was relieved when a long weekend came.

One particular weekend, around six weeks prior to my due date, I began to experience pain and as soon as we got back to the office, Dr. Morris examined me. I noticed that he kept listening to the heartbeat, then he yelled, "Tillie, come here." He held up 2 fingers and as she listened, I knew. I was having twins and I was in labor. It was an exciting time for everyone. Two bassinets were set up in the delivery room at the hospital and we waited. I was in labor for four days before our twins were born, premature. They were in the incubator for two weeks and I was on bed rest for a week before I could see them. I remember crying, begging the doctor to see them. I kept telling him, "I want to see my babies, I want to see what they look like," he said "I'll tell you what they look like, they look like two little red pigs," to which I cried even more.

When he finally let me bring them home (early), I soon realized what an overwhelming job it was. Not only was I unfamiliar with babies, being the mother of premature babies was more than a full time job. The only help I had was when Jack got home from work.

The babies had to be fed every three hours and it usually took an hour to feed them, plus making bottles (making formula and sterilizing bottles) and the endless job of changing diapers. I depended on the doctors for advice, as I had no experience in taking care of anything but baby animals and never premature ones. Jack and I were unbelievably tired. There were nights of falling asleep with babies on the bed between us, cold bottles hanging out of their mouths. I finally tried sitting in a straight chair to feed them, only to find a baby sliding down my legs, almost on the floor.

The twins' first trip to the doctor's office was quite an experience. Dr. Tillie had the firm belief that babies should not be given pacifiers and emphasized that to me about the twins. However, in the process of giving them their first shots, the babies got so upset that Dr. Tillie finally said " give those babies a pacifier."

Years later, after Dr. Tillie retired and moved to Chapel Hill, she would occasionally come back to her beloved home at CCNC for a week or so at a time.

When she did, several of my friends and I would stay with her, day and night as long as she was there.

Her favorite place in the house was sitting in her comfy chair, in the den, watching the birds and squirrels, eating and playing in the back yard. She would laugh and call them "little monkeys."

The last time I took care of her, I took her to Hoffman to visit an old friend. Before we left, her friend told us about a new restaurant that had opened up in Hoffman. She told us that the food was very good, so we decided to check it out while we were there. As I followed her friend's directions, I was still confused as we arrived at our destination- - we were at a BP station! Dr. Tillie didn't seem at all surprised, so I went along with the plan. When we walked in, Dr. Tillie went straight to the case where the food was displayed.

She was excited that they had fried chicken, home fries and an assortment of other fried foods. As I sat there and watched her eat this simple meal of greasy food on a paper plate in an old wooden booth at a service station, I was amazed at the sheer enjoyment she showed. On the way home, she told me how much she had enjoyed the day. That night, she called her family to tell them about the best fried chicken she had ever eaten, at a restaurant in Hoffman.

High Cost of Guilt

It was when I was in the hospital, having my tonsils removed that I received the first and only doll that I remember as a child. I thought she was the most beautiful doll that I had ever seen. Her fragile, ceramic face was encased in a delicate white lace cap and she had on a lovely white dress with lace on it. I treasured my doll above anything I had. One day, the unthinkable happened. I walked into the pantry and much of my horror, I saw Don, my nephew raising a hammer over my doll's head. I screamed as he brought the hammer down on her face, and with a crushing blow, I saw her beautiful head crumble in what seems like a million pieces. I was hysterical. I jumped on him and started beating him with my fists as hard as I could. For a moment, the anger that I felt for him overpowered the sick feeling I had when I looked at what had been my treasured doll.

However, his screaming brought me back to reality. Suddenly, I was afraid I had hurt him and would be in big trouble.

You see, Don was also fragile from an accident which resulted in a brain injury when he was four years old.

By then Don had recovered from his accident but he was still pampered and in the family's eyes "could do no wrong". Since I knew I would be the one in trouble, even though he had destroyed my doll, I begged him not to "tell on me" for hitting him, he just screamed that much louder, "I'm telling"; he did and I got in trouble.

My younger son, Jeff had a different approach to being in trouble. One day he called me at work and asked if I could come home for lunch, When I asked him why, he replied, "I accidentally killed a red bird with my bow and arrow. I know I'm in trouble, so could you come home and give me my punishment now?"

Another incident involved Mark and Kelly. Evidently, they were arguing and Mark was chasing Kelly. He saw a hair spray can on the ground, picked it up and threw it at her. The can hit her leg and immediately the blood started pouring from her leg.

He realized he was in big trouble, so he started begging her "not to tell", even promising her "a million dollars" if she wouldn't. Kelly still says she has a million dollar scar that Mark owes her for.

There is a high price for guilt, even though, at times short lived.

Forest Fire

It was a blustery day. We hadn't had rain for weeks and the ground was bone dry. I had no idea what a day like this would hold for everyone around.

The first thing I noticed was what appeared to be a black cloud. I thought it strange that the cloud seemed to be moving faster than a normal cloud. Then I smelled smoke and I instantly knew. Forest Fire! And it was moving toward my house! Soon, I started getting phone calls and neighbors stopping by to tell me that the area was being evacuated. I tried to reach my husband at work but he had already left. I knew he was trying to come home.

I had to make a decision, whether to leave or stay. I thought about it for a few minutes; then I knew. I would stay and protect my home. My neighbors thought I was crazy but I was determined. I told the children to go in the house, take the cats and dogs and stay there. I grabbed the longest hose I could find and a ladder, turned on the water and climbed up on the roof.

I started spraying down the roof and as I watched the smoke move closer I questioned the decision I had made. And as the sky grew darker I almost came down off the roof. Then suddenly the cloud seem to stop and I began to see some light peeking through. My legs were still shaking as I breathed a sigh of relief and climbed down from the roof and thanked God for stopping the fire that could have destroyed our home.

Drifting Too Far From Shore

Though the children loved the beach, trips to the coast, for our large family were few and far between. Building sandcastles, playing football, and sunbathing on the beach, as well as riding the waves were the children's favorite activities. Even the food tasted better with a little sand mixed in! Many times we would leave early in the morning, spend the day at the beach and come home late that night; sandy, sticky and sleepy.

One summer, while everyone was involved in their own activities on the beach, as I counted heads, I realized a child was missing. Finally, I spotted Kelly, way off on the horizon, on her float, in very deep water. Without realizing the danger, she had drifted out past the waves, into seemingly still waters. I tried yelling to her but she couldn't hear me and since there was no life guard or any other adults around, and even though I wasn't a swimmer, I raced toward her.

When I was finally able to get her attention and reach her, on my tip toes, I pulled a scared little girl in to shore. It was only when we were back on the beach, that the reality of what had just happened hit me, I collapsed on the sand, weeping and thanking God for saving my daughter.

Dishes

Growing up, no one hated washing dishes more than I did. There were so many others things on the farm that deserved my attention, I thought. I didn't like drying and putting the dishes away either. One day, in an effort to finish the dishes in a hurry without having to dry them, I stacked the dishes too high in the drainer. Just as I had carefully placed that last item on the mountain of dishes, pots, pans and silverware and turned around, I heard a crash behind me. As I looked down, I saw Mama's favorite cast iron frying pan, on the floor, with the handle broken off. I wanted to run and hide but as I stood there in shock, staring down at the broken pieces, Mama and Daddy walked in the kitchen. Needless to say, Mama expressed her disappointment in me while Daddy stood by in silence. After what seemed to be an eternity of Daddy carefully "studying" the pieces, he said, "I can fix it". Weeks went by and I thought the frying pan incident was forgotten when Daddy came in and told me he had a surprise for me.

Thinking it was one of his usual surprises of candy or gum I was curious about such a large brown bag. To my delight, as I carefully opened the bag, I saw the most beautiful cast iron frying pan, whose handle had been repaired with what appeared to be gold (Daddy had the handle soldered together in a copper color). Finally, I felt vindicated when I realized that Mama was satisfied with her "new" frying pan. After many years, I am now the proud owner of that frying pan and use it frequently.

My children must have hated washing dishes as much as I did. They would do almost anything to get out of that chore. Years later I found dishes in the woods behind the house that only after many years did I learn the real story behind the missing dishes. When they suddenly realized it was time for "Mom" to be home from work and they hadn't even started washing the dishes, rather than get caught, they hid them. Sometimes, I would get home from work and find the neighbor boy, at the sink, washing dishes, standing in a chair because he was too short to reach the sink. Someone had bribed him, with who knows what.

One day my oldest son; Mark, the son who hated washing dishes more than the other three, came rolling a dishwasher in. When I asked him about it, he told me it was his gift to me and when it was his turn to wash dishes, just turn it on. No more washing dishes for him, he said.

Thank God for dishwashers!

A Christmas Play

One year our church undertook the enormous task of putting on a live nativity play. None of us had ever attempted anything like this, but as we all began to catch the vision, the excitement mounted. As the characters were chosen and arrangements were made to procure the animals, things began to fall in place. What we didn't take into consideration was the temperament of animals and the extremely cold weather.

The night finally arrived when our big production would start. You would have thought it was Hollywood as all the children rehearsed their parts while drinking hot chocolate in the basement of the church. In spite of a few glitches with the animals, we had a huge turn out and received rave reviews and to this day, the year we presented the Christmas story is one of my family's favorite memories, especially about the four of them exchanging each others roles.

Are We There Yet?

Just hearing the phrase "Are we there yet?"
brings back memories of family trips. No
matter if it was a long or short trip, we didn't
have to wait long to see who was going to be
the first to ask, "Are we there yet?" or "I
need to go to the bathroom", even if the last
word out of my mouth, before leaving the
house was: "Everybody, make sure you go
to the bathroom, so we don't have to stop."

Finally, we'd be on our way, but with four
kids, within three years apart in age,
crammed into the back seat of the car, it
didn't take long for the complaining to start:
"she pulled my hair," "he hit me," "she
breathed on me," "it's hot in here," "I'm
cold," "I'm hungry," "I'm thirsty," "Are we
there yet?" and of course, "I've got to go to
the bathroom."

On day trips to the beach, the ride home was
usually quieter. We had spent the day on the
beach and everybody was tired, worn out,
sunburned and sticky from salt and sand.

It didn't take too long for the four of them to be fast asleep, all in one pile, finally peaceful, and I could finally breathe a sigh of relief, enjoying a quiet ride home.

The Flying Motorcycle

It seemed to be a typical Sunday afternoon in the neighborhood; a beautiful summer day, when most of the neighborhood would gather to ride bikes, motorcycles or a start a game of baseball or football, but that day was different. There was excitement in the air; most of the guys, adults included, were in our front yard. Junior, who lived at the end of the dirt road beside our house, was showing off his brand-new Honda dirt bike. Since Jeff has some experience riding mini-bikes, Junior didn't hesitate when Jeff asked to ride his new bike. Jeff hopped on the bike, started it up and took off down the road.

I was sitting on the couch in the living room, reading, when I just happened to look up. I couldn't believe my eyes! Was that a motorcycle that I saw flying across the road and down the embankment? Who was on it? It looked like Jeff.

As I was running out the door, I was telling myself "It couldn't be Jeff – he doesn't have a motorcycle." Just then I saw a car coming to a screeching stop beside the highway and a lady, screaming, jumping out of the car. Other cars and campers were stopping along the highway, as well as neighbors running in the same direction that I was, down the embankment (which was around 7 feet deep) to see what had happened. As we scrambled down the hill we saw a figure emerging from the bushes. It **was** Jeff, dazed, pushing the motorcycle, repeating over and over, "I'm OK, I'm not hurt." Then I saw Junior running down the road, "what have you done to my motorcycle?" Jeff's answer was, "It's OK. See, it's still running."

When everyone got back to the house and checked Jeff and the motorcycle out for damages, the amazing story was revealed. Jeff's friend, Junior had just gotten his first, brand new motorcycle and in showing it off, offered to let Jeff drive it. In his hurried instructions, and Jeff's excitement to try it out, Junior forgot to tell Jeff how to operate the brakes.

It was only when Jeff was racing at full speed down the dirt road toward the highway that he realized he didn't know where the brakes were.

As Jeff, still pale and shaking, explained that he had just planned to ride past our house and wave, wasn't accustomed to the gears or brakes on this bike, nor how fast it was. He said, when he passed the house, he realized he couldn't stop. He saw the cars on the road and just knew he was going to die, saying that his life passed before him and he froze. He was racing at full speed down the dirt road toward the highway, with no place to go but straight ahead and down the embankment. He said that if he hadn't kept the gas at full throttle, he would have crashed into the car that was passing by on the highway. The hysterical lady in the car told us that she was so sure he had hit him, she had waited for the impact.

It was just another exciting day in the neighborhood. Jeff, nor Junior's bike even had a scratch on them! No hard feelings – everybody forgiven, including the "almost-new" Honda dirt bike!

In spite of a few more gray hairs, I couldn't help but chuckle at the thought of seeing "a flying motorcycle!"

Motorcycle Mania

The fascination with motorcycles in our neighborhood started in the early seventies. Several of the families had motorcycles, including our family. There were motorcycles of all sizes and shapes, from street bikes to trail bikes. It wasn't uncommon on a Sunday afternoon to hear the "VA-room" of several bikes cranking up, in unison, preparing for a leisurely ride. The sound of the kids and their bikes, though, was a daily occurrence, as they raced through the trails they had created.

In spite of their "rules of the trails," there were still accidents, from time to time and some of them were serious collisions, which required numerous trips to the ER. Through the years, more of the details of these accidents have been revealed. One such accident, involved my two sons, Mark and Jeff.

In this accident, Jeff's face was bloodied pretty bad, so Mark took his white t-shirt off, cleaned Jeff's face up, buried the shirt and they vowed not to tell me about the accident.

Another serious accident involved Jeff and my two nephews, Dale and Rex, in a head-on collision. The three of them had been riding on the trails near Dale and Rex's house (without my knowledge), when they realized that Jeff's bike was almost out of gas. Dale took the bike and went for gas. While he was gone, Jeff and Rex decided to follow him, but Dale was already on his way back. As they rounded the curve near the lake, the two bikes collided. Somehow, the boys got back to the house, even though Jeff's bike was so twisted, he couldn't ride it. He began calling me on the phone, but I couldn't understand him – he wasn't making sense (later at the hospital I found out that he had a concussion, a ripped up lip and a broken tooth). I didn't know where he was but I suspected he was with Dale and Rex, so I got in the car, sped up the highway and found them.

There were several other accidents, but none that severe, UNTIL June 9, 2007. Jeff was riding a Yamaha YZ250 at the sand pit on Dale's property. He had gone over this particular jump many times, but this time when he started to jump across, the front wheel of the bike got caught in the deep sand and caused the bike to turn, sending him over the handle bars. He landed on his head at the bottom of the sand pit; the bike on top of him. The temperature was 96 degrees in the shade; he was alone and in excruciating pain. He struggled to get up and was finally able to reach for his phone to call for help. In spite of his pain and thirst, he continued to move, trying to find some shade and amazingly was able to start the motorcycle before help arrived. Soon, family and rescue vehicles were on the scene, including an air flight helicopter and he was painfully airlifted to the hospital in Chapel Hill.

Vertebrae seven, eight and nine in Jeff's back were broken, as well as multiple broken ribs, and both of his lungs were collapsed.

Even though he was in a body cast for three months, he was soon back at work and before long, back on his motorcycle.

And he's still riding.

Three Surgeries in a Week

As I recall, it was late summer almost a year after the twins (Mark and Lynne) started school. They were actually 5 years old when they started to school since their birthdays were in September. It had been a difficult winter with the two of them bringing home all the childhood diseases: chicken pox, mumps, measles, as well as tonsillitis, ear infections, and colds, etc. For months at a time, the whole family was sick, passing around whatever the latest sickness happened to be. Ms. Jenkins, Mark and Lynne's first grade teacher came to our house on a regular basis and tutored them, in bed.

Since Lynne and Kelly were having so many problems with their tonsils and Mark, with so many ear infections, the doctors suggested surgery for all of them. Lynne and Kelly had tonsillectomies at the same time at what is now Moore Regional Hospital in Pinehurst.

Their surgeries went well and the three of us settled into a room with two hospital beds. They seemed to be enjoying all the special attention they were receiving from the nurses; all the ice cream and Jell-O they could eat and the undivided attention they were receiving from "Mama" until bedtime, when no one wanted to share their bed with "Mama" then.

The next day, after the girls were released from the hospital and getting settled at home, I received a call from Duke Hospital telling me that Mark was scheduled for surgery the next day. Arrangements were quickly made for the girls to be cared by my sister, Ana, and my dad. Jeff (3 years old) was taken to good friends, the Shoes. It should be noted that Jeff had never been away from me and was extremely unhappy that I was leaving him. He went so far as to "disown" me as his mother, after we all returned home, telling me he didn't have a mother. It was quite an adjustment period for him.

As soon as everyone was settled into their temporary locations, Jack (my husband) took Mark and me to Duke Hospital in

Durham for Mark's surgery (tubes in his ears.)

As soon as we were settled in, Jack left. Mark was assigned a room with another little boy around his age and was content with the situation until the nurse came in and told me I had to leave, that visiting hours were over. Mark and I were both upset. I explained to the nurse that I wasn't leaving, that I would stay in the lobby, if they wouldn't let me stay in his room. I tried to remain calm as I left the room, telling Mark I would be back as soon as they would let me. The mother of the other boy told me that she had a mother-child room and would be with both the boys all night and would take care of Mark as well as her son. Somewhat relieved, I left the room, but, as I looked back, I saw that Mark was crying, which broke my heart.

I went to the lobby and found a secluded spot and closed my eyes, only to be roused by a security officer telling me I had to leave. When I explained my situation to him and told him I had no place to go, he took me to a nice lady seated behind a desk who gave me information about a home near the hospital.

She explained to me that I could spend the night there and a bus could take me there and bring me back to the hospital early the next morning.

Before long I had taken a short bus trip to a lovely part of town and was being greeted by another nice lady at her very "homey feeling" home. The next thing I remember after I had taken a bath, put my pajamas on and my head hit the pillow, I was waking up, refreshed and on my way back to the hospital.

When I arrived back in Mark's room, I realized I had worried for nothing, as he and the other little boy were playing and the mother said they had all slept well.

Soon, Mark was taken to surgery and I was told that I would be called as soon as he was out of surgery. While he was gone, I went to the cafeteria to get some breakfast. I felt like a "country bumpkin" wandering around the hospital. The contraption that I called the "walk-through gate with the bar across it" was the most confusing and frustrating. When I finally asked someone about it and was told "just walk through it" still didn't make sense.

I thought to myself, "How do you walk through a bar?" I think I finally climbed over it!

When I returned from my excursion, I checked with the nurse about Mark's surgery and again was told that I would be called when the surgery was over. I didn't ask again, but was really getting worried when my brother, U.T. arrived and couldn't believe that I hadn't heard anything. He, then, went to the desk and talked with the nurse and soon I got a call that he was fine and would be back in his room shortly. Evidently, they had forgotten him, because within minutes he was being wheeled into his room. When I first saw him, he was a frightening sight; dried blood all around his nose, mouth and ears and he was crying. Soon, he was cleaned up and happy until visiting hours were over again. But by the next day, he was released, the other children picked up and everyone home and recuperating from the three surgeries within a very long and tiring week.

Sleeping with a Stranger

It was 1980 and my son, Mark, was in the Navy, stationed at Norfolk, VA. He was preparing to have surgery on his hand at Portsmouth Naval Hospital.

I was at my Aunt Lett's house and was telling her that I would like to be with Mark while he had his surgery but I didn't have a place to stay and couldn't afford a hotel room.

It was at that time that Aunt Lett told me about my cousin who lived in Norfolk. She began to come up with a plan for me to stay with her and before I knew what was happening she had called Lois, my cousin, and was handing me the phone. After an awkward introduction, explaining my dilemma, plans were made for our visit.

When Mark and I arrived at the address Lois had given me, I was surprised that we were at a very tall, high rise apartment building.

After arriving at what seemed to be the top floor, we were graciously greeted by my cousin, Lois, in her tiny little apartment. As we chatted and Lois showed me around, Mark disappeared, then reappeared in a few minutes carrying his luggage. That was when I realized that Mark was planning to stay at Lois' tiny little apartment too! I panicked, realizing that Lois only had one bedroom, with a double bed! I quickly took Lois into her bedroom, shut the door and explained my dilemma. Without a blink of an eye, she again came to my rescue and quickly replied "Mark can sleep on the couch and you can sleep with me." My first thought was, "I don't know this woman! She's a stranger!" but I quickly recovered and replied, "Thank you, Thank you!"

For the next few days, Mark and I experienced what love and real hospitality were, as this older lady, living in a retirement home, took in two total strangers and treated them like royalty.

As we traveled home a few days later, after a successful surgery, we reminisced about our adventure with a modern-day "Good Samaritan!"

The Old Sycamore

At the time, the little twig of a sycamore
tree seemed rather insignificant when
Daddy brought her to our new house
and planted her in the back yard. He
told the children, "As you grow up, you'll
see this tree grow up to be a huge tree."

Years have come and gone since that
day. No longer are the children climbing
her mighty branches, cutting their
names into her trunk, or jumping and
rolling in piles of leaves she
accumulated. The "old girl" gave us
shade for picnics, as well as shade for
numerous dogs whose houses were
nestled at the base of her trunk.
Squirrels, and all kinds of birds made
their nests in that old tree. Even snakes
have been seen wrapped around her
trunk. Though the peals of laughter have
stopped as the children have grown up
and left home, and there are no dogs in
the houses, the memories remain.

The majestic old tree began to "feel her age" a few years ago and started losing a few branches. Then, more and bigger branches began to fall. I think she was preparing me for the day when she was ready to go. The old tree that had given so much was dead. She was still proud and stately as her massive trunk was cut and fell to the ground, seeming to shake the earth around it. Her silhouette against the changing colors of the sunset was still beautiful. Now, the only traces of the magnificent tree are the neat sections of wood, precisely cut, lying where they fell. Even though there is a void where the sycamore stood, memories of the joy she brought still remain.

The Old Sycamore was 48 years old when she passed away on December 27, 2011.

A Grandfather's Legacy

If I could spend an afternoon with one member of my extended family, it would be my step grandson. If I had the opportunity to spend an afternoon with him, I would tell him about his grandfather, who died before he was born. I would tell him how much his grandfather would love having such a handsome, smart grandson. He would be so pleased that his son had chosen a good wife and mother to his grandchildren. He also would be pleased that they are involved in church and have a beautiful home. He would love the fact that his grandson now has a little sister, in spite of the fact that sometimes he might want to send her back.

I would tell him about his grandfather's health problems and the fact that he didn't drink and wouldn't want him to. I would also tell him that he blamed his heart attack on smoking and would never want his grandchildren to smoke or do drugs.

I would tell him that even though his grandfather isn't here, someday, when he gets to heaven, he will be able to meet him.

Christmas In Prison

One of my most memorable Christmases was the year all my family was out of town. I was working at the prison at the time and naturally my thoughts were with the inmates who were away from their families. They were young men, many of them separated from family and friends for the first time. Whether they were guilty or not, loneliness can affect anyone, particularly during the holidays.

Anyway, I decided, rather than stay at home and eat alone, I'd have Christmas dinner with the inmates at the prison. The inmates seemed shocked to see me pick up my tray and sit down at a table with some of them. After they got over the shock of my being here, the atmosphere seemed to change as we talked and laughed and ate one of the worst Christmas dinners I had ever tasted.

The Barrier Island Adventure

It was sometime around the late 1980's. I was working at the prison hospital when Eileen (a friend from work) and I decided to take her son, Eric and my grandson, Justin and head to the coast for an adventure. Even though I had called the campground and asked that my camper be pulled out of storage, we still had to set up the camper in the dark. By the time we had dinner and went to bed, we didn't have much time for sleeping, as we had to leave early the next morning for our excursion.

We had seen the ad in the local newspaper, advertising the trip to "Bulls Island," one of the barrier islands off the coast of South Carolina. The advertisement didn't give very much information, but it sounded like fun. We packed our lunch, which included sandwiches, snacks and cokes (no water), suntan lotion and we were ready for our adventure.

When we arrived at the pick-up point, we met a number of other people who were also going to the island. As we climbed in the boat and got on our way, the driver asked us to decide which side of the island we wanted to go to.

As he described the choices, the "beach side" sounded more appealing to us, since it had a beach, and access to seashells, that could only be found on that side of the island. We noticed that everyone got off at the first stop except two other ladies and us, which I thought, a little strange at the time. Later, I realized why!

On his way to drop us off on the far side of the island, the driver gave us further instructions: "don't go near the alligators – that's the noise you hear, and don't go near the wolves, the state raises these almost extinct red wolves here on the island – they are in the other direction"

and there is a path through
the forest to the other side of
the island, but don't try to go
through there, it's
dangerous!" and "I will be
back around 4:00 pm to pick
you up. Be ready – I won't be
coming back again."

All I could think of was, take
me back now! What do you
mean; you're leaving us out
here alone?!!! But I didn't
want to be a bad sport, so I
crawled out of the boat and
onto the beach. For the next
several hours, we explored the
island, picked up all sorts of
unusual shells, climbed over
huge dead trees at what is
called "Boneyard Beach"
(near the path to the other
side), ate our lunch and drank
hot cokes.

Hot, tired and wishing for some shade and cool water (or even warm water), we could hear the alligators "barking" and heard the wolves howling! We were ready to get out of that place! Then we noticed a dark, menacing looking cloud that was growing larger by the minute, that seemed to be heading our way. Eileen and I were frantic but trying to stay calm for the sake of the boys. We found the other ladies and discussed our options: should we try the path to the other side, since it wasn't time for our ride or should be wait, hope and pray that our driver would realize our predicament and pick us up early?

We chose the latter option and before too long we heard the sound of a motor and saw the boat speeding through the water.

As we dragged our tired, sandy, aching bodies (and parched throats), our shells and driftwood onto the boat, we couldn't get away from that island fast enough, as we outran the storm and headed home.

That night, back at the camper, after we had our showers, dinner and cool water, we recalled our adventure on Bulls Island and compared ourselves to Robinson Crusoe.

Old Treasures

How different each of us are. Different
tastes, different looks, different ideas – even
different finger prints – no two alike. God
designed us that way. We are unique. How
uninteresting this world would be if we were
all alike, looked alike, had the same ideas.
How boring!

Some folks enjoy changes, they are
constantly moving their furniture from one
place to another. They even move pieces out
and start a totally new theme. These people
usually readily accept new fads and fashions
while others are slow to accept change of
any kind.

These other folks, as I'll call them, are like
me. Slow to accept change. I like old things.
I like to restore the broken, to repair them
and return them to their original, useful
state. I like the old, odd pieces of furniture
that we were given when we were married,
that I painted, and even though some of the
pieces are chipped, the drawers need some

work, they don't exactly match, but to me, they're beautiful, they're treasures.

The people that like change may have beautiful things, beautiful homes with all the changes, but as for me I'm happy with the old, comfortable, homey stuff, things that have been around for a lifetime. Like my mother's ring. I thought it was lost. I had searched and searched for it when I was younger as well as asking folks what happened to it. No one seemed to know, until a few years ago, when my sister and I were talking and I mentioned that I thought Mama was buried with her wedding ring or someone took it. To my surprise, she replied, "I have it – do you want it? After all this time, there it was, in a little black jewelry box, just as beautiful as ever. As I slid it on my finger, along with my other rings that I plan to pass down to my children, I was amazed, not only at the mystery being solved, but I now have a treasure of a lifetime, the legacy of the old stuff that I hold dear.

The Almost Indestructible Pansy

Because of my fondness of pansies, I filled
numerous containers of brilliant colored
pansies this past fall. I didn't give them
much attention after that, except for
watering them, feeding them a little fertilizer
now and then, and chasing the squirrels
away (their favorite place to hide acorns.)
The day after our big February snowfall
(around five inches of snow with a topping
of ice), as I looked out my kitchen window,
admiring all the shapes covered up with
snow and ice, I noticed something yellow
peeking out from a basket hanging under the
gazebo. Upon further investigation, as I
checked the pots of pansies, I saw beautiful,
little faces struggling for a ray of sunshine
from underneath mounds of snow and ice. I
remarked at the endurance of these tiny little
plants: their strength, their determination,
their resilience.

No matter what they go through—wind, rain, ice, snow, freezing temperatures, sometimes even being crushed, battling the elements, whatever they have to face—they just pop back up and let their little faces shine, reaching for the sun. Then, when the temperatures begin to warm up, they really let their beauty shine, as if what they went through during the hard winter caused them to be even stronger and more beautiful.

So it is with us. Just as the squirrel is the enemy to the pansies, our enemy, the devil, would like to crush us, especially after going through a winter of difficulties, but like the pansies, if we will just turn our faces toward the Son and allow Him to bring us through, we will be stronger, more resilient, and more beautiful as His light shines through us.

The Neeley's

I met Mr. and Mrs. Thomas Neeley through friends and they quickly became my friends as well. They lived in the mountains of North Carolina and their home was always open to anyone who, passing through the area needed a place to stay. They entertained people from all over the world, and they, especially had a heart for missionaries, as they were retired from the mission field.

I felt "at home" immediately upon entering their humble two story house. My friends and I were assigned to an upstairs bedrooms, along with our bed linens. As we walked down the spacious hallway I noticed that each bedroom had a biblical name, such as Bethany, Jerusalem, above each door. The bedrooms were neat, clean, like the rest of the house, with just the essentials, a bed, and a nightstand.

I soon realized that everything about the Neeleys' household was on a strict schedule.

Every meal was cooked by Mrs. Neeley in their rather crowded kitchen with a long wooden table;
strictly by the weekly menu – every week the same, at the same time and you had "better be on time." Mr. Neeley cut the wood for the large wood stove and kept the wood box filled with big, heavy chunks of wood. Shelves around the walls of the kitchen held all sorts of herbs which Mrs. Neeley harvested and used for cooking. I was horrified when Mrs. Neeley told me that she ate one poke berry a day for her health. I told her that I eat the greens but I had been told the berries were poison. She replied, "Oh, no, they are why I'm in such good health."

An in-depth Bible study was held regularly in the Neeley home and every guest was expected to participate. As Mr. Neeley taught the lesson he would call on each person to read a portion of scripture and discuss it. At first, I was terrified but he was a very good teacher, open to everyone's explanations and ideas and soon I realized I was enjoying the lively discussions and learned during that experience how much fun it is to study the Bible.

In fact, I thank God for the Neeleys and a lasting impression they made on me.

The Ride of a Lifetime

Imagine being in a foreign country in an old, rickety car driven by a strange man who couldn't speak English. I vividly remember my friend's husband's words as I left Friedburg Military Base, where he was stationed, "Don't get in that car with him, Peggy, he might be a terrorist." Why didn't I listen to him? What is going to happen to me? I don't even know how to use German money, or a phone, I thought to myself. About that time, I panicked even more when I began to see signs to Hanau pointing to the right and the driver kept making left turns. I desperately tried using sign language to let him know he was going in the wrong direction, to which he kept replying "Nein!" Just as I thought I would have a heart attack, he turned onto a ramp which led up to a huge highway and I heard myself screaming, "Autobahn!"

This crazed driver just looked at me, smiled and repeated Autobahn, as he put the gas pedal to the floor. As my head and body was jerked backward, I watched the numbers on the speedometer disappear and the ride of a lifetime began.

Trying to relax was almost impossible, but as I watched cars and trucks flying by the raggedy, old Mercedes, I tried not to think about how fast we must be going. As I attempted to settle down a little and get my thoughts together, I remembered something the driver was trying to tell David before we left the base, that since I was the only one who showed up at Friedburg, he was taking me to another military base to meet the bus and the rest of my group that would be going to Paris. Since it was an "Express Tour," we were scheduled to leave around midnight and return the next night around the same time. I found out later that my driver had to make this trip after he had gotten off work and wasn't too happy about it.

After about an hour of bouncing, bumping, jerking, swerving and being scared practically out of my mind, we "caught up" with the other bus, literally. We had been sitting at the base for about a half hour, waiting, when we saw the bus coming (we were on the wrong side of the base) and it didn't stop. After chasing the bus down, I jumped out of that monster car and ran up to the bus drivers and said, "I've never been so glad to find someone who speaks English!" When they laughed, I realized they were German too, and spoke very little English! It didn't matter though, I wasn't the only American on that bus and I was going to Paris!

Superman of the Laundromat

Upon entering a laundromat, you will find rows of washing machines and dryers, a money-changing machine and a vending machine that dispenses whatever you need to operate the machines, such as, washing powder, dryer sheets, etc., (if machines work.)

Inside you will find an assortment of people, from all walks of life; busy working on stacks of clothes. I often wonder, what brought them to the laundromat? Was it a broken-down washing machine at home that brought the lady in the second row of machines? Is the gentleman with a week's worth of jeans and shirts a worker from out of town? Does the young lady with the three little children not have a washer and dryer at home, having to do her weekly laundry at the laundromat?

You can easily distinguish the first-timers from the regulars. Some immediately begin chatting with each other as if they are old friends; some sit quietly reading books, while others just walk in, put their clothes in the washers, leave, and come back later, without acknowledging anyone.

I walked into the laundromat with my friend's over-sized comforter in my arms. I forgot the clothes basket. Then I tried to fit the comforter in a smaller machine, finally forcing it into a giant money-guzzling washer. Next, I had to have $5.00 worth of quarters to put in that big, old, hungry beast. At that point, a gentleman sitting in front of the vending machine told me that the detergent machine was broken. So, I lugged the big, old comforter back to the car and headed to Big Lots to find a "small" box of detergent and a laundry basket. When I looked at the price of the laundry basket and the detergent, I decided against the flimsy $10.00 laundry basket and walked out with a "bargain" jug of detergent, telling myself I could find something in the car to lay the comforter on.

(By the way, the "tinfoil looking" windshield visor worked just fine for the comforter to rest on!)

When I got back to the laundromat, I stuffed the comforter back into another hungry beast, fed it a good meal of quarters and headed off to get a sandwich at the sub shop next door, while I was waiting. As I leisurely sat eating my sandwich and watching folks passing by, I saw a man walk into the laundromat wearing what appeared to be "ladies" white Capri pants that were very short and skintight. He seemed to be in a hurry, but his pants were so tight, he was walking as if he couldn't bend his legs. As I sat munching on my sandwich, reflecting what I had just seen, out the door burst the same man, but, to my amazement, he was wearing a pair of beige slacks that fit perfectly! As I burst out laughing, I said to myself, *IT'S SUPERMAN!* When I went back to pick up the comforter, I looked around and tried to imagine which one of these women did the white slacks that SUPERMAN had on belong to? Were those slacks his mother's or his sister's? And which clothes basket did he pull his SUPERMAN outfit; the one he changed into so quickly – out of?

Jenny's Elusive Cake

As we made our plans for our Easter family get together, I had an idea! Since Jenny had just completed her studies in Columbia, SC for her Master's Degree, we should celebrate! I could bake a cake and decorate it. Kristen and I talked about how to decorate the cake and she came up with the idea "You mastered it" for the wording. I went shopping for the ingredients and my plan was to bake the cake on Saturday morning and decorate it after I got back from church that night. The plan was going fairly well at first; I had a little scare when the middle of the cake rose up like a mountain, then settled down and flattened out, so I covered it with tin foil and left for the church. When I started assembling the ingredients for the icing. That's when I realized I didn't have enough confectioner sugar for the icing and the decorations and it was too late to go back into town to buy more. So, I went online and looked at every recipe I could find for a solution. Finally, I compromised; I cut the icing recipe back in order to have enough icing to barely cover the cake and decorate it. Then, when I pulled out my decorator kit, there was no bag to put the icing in. So I quickly resorted to "old faithful", my antique decorator contraption, which only has one tip. She's messy, and sometimes the writing is rather sloppy, but she gets the job done. In spite of all the challenges, I was satisfied with the finished product. I was sure Jenny would appreciate it and maybe get a laugh out of: "Congrats Jenny – You mastered it."

So, Easter arrived and I hurriedly packed the car, checked my list and reminded myself "don't forget the cake, don't forget the cake" just before my last load to the car. Just as I turned onto the Carthage exit, I looked at my watch – how could it be almost 2:00? I couldn't believe, after all the planning I was going to be late. I sped up a little.

I looked at my watch again just as I was pulling in at the barn – it was 2:00 pm – right on time.

When I opened the back door and reached for the cooler, I realized something was missing.

My heart sunk – where was the cake? How could I forget the cake? I couldn't believe it! What was I going to do?

First, I called my neighbor, Sharon, who verified that the cake was actually on the kitchen table. That's when I decided to go back to get it. After much objections, I was on the way out the door when Mark asked me what I was doing. When he heard my story, he overruled me and went for the cake.

About an hour and a half later, when I saw my son walk in with my pitiful Coca Cola cake with green icing, he was my hero. He saved the day, with Jenny's elusive cake and my dream of honoring my granddaughter on her special day!

Helen

There once was a man named Mark who had two cats. Their names were Chevy and Chrysler, and they lived at Mark's shop. They loved attention and were always ready to have their backs scratched anytime he had a free moment. They were happy spending their days watching Mark work and their nights, keeping watch over the shop.

But Mark's shop was a busy place and when he got home, at night, he was lonely. Then one day, Helen came into Mark's life and came to live with him at his house. Helen was a beauty; very lovable and Mark found her fascinating. She especially loved to stroke Mark's hair after his shower at night. Helen made herself at home at Mark's house and Mark enjoyed her company too. Mark realized that since Helen had come to live with him, his loneliness had left.

Mark wanted to introduce Chevy and
Chrysler to Helen, but after he found out
that Helen had shown some jealousy
tendencies and was prone to fight, he
realized he couldn't, after all, you see …

Helen is a CAT.

Elvis!

Funny, the things you hear or don't hear
when you're losing your hearing. The things
you want to hear, you don't and the things
you don't want to hear (like background
noises) you do. Frustrating!

When in a situation such as this and you can
hear absolutely nothing, someone has
suggested that you just nod your head and
say, "Uh huh, yes, that's right."

Other people think, on the other hand, the
higher the volume or pitch, the better they
think you can hear. So, if you ask them to
repeat something, they yell in your ear, as if
you're totally deaf and again, you can't hear
what they are saying.

It's actually very funny, the things you think
you hear. If you repeat back what you
thought you heard, it is not at all what the
person said!

Carrying on phone conversations, particularly with some cellphones can really be a hassle. And if both parties have their phones on speaker – forget it – it reminds me of years ago talking with my sons while they were on aircraft carriers out at sea or a CB radio, when you had to remember to say "over," before the other person could hear what you were saying.

An example of a typical conversation happened today, when my cellphone rang and I couldn't understand anything the man was saying. Finally, I understood him say his name was "Elvis." The only Elvis I could think of was "Elvis Presley," I was totally confused. When I finally realized who he was and why he had called, the conversation was almost over and I was saying "Uh huh, yes, that's right."

When I "hung up the phone" I had a good laugh, saying to myself, "I just talked to Elvis!"

Better to laugh than cry!

Dogs, Medicine, Syringes, Pills and The Little Red Card.

The dogs, one blind (that's Meika); another, a diabetic with thyroid problems (that's Murphy); another that licks constantly (that's Buddy); also, a cat that throws up (that's Ginger.) What's that all add up to? Trips to the vet, NC State Vet School, The Equine Center and the little red card!!! They all know me and my little red card. One of the attendants told me she saw a little red card like mine and thought someone had stolen my card. What's wrong with this picture?

Let's talk about these meds – Eight different ones - it's a full time job, just keeping them straight. Am I in training for something? No, I'm too old for that.

Now, how much do I give of this new medicine? When? Which antibiotic goes to which dog? Was the Baytril for Murphy and Doxycycline for Meika or visa versa? Did you say <u>two</u> Prednisones?? Oh, no, more pee papers! How many times have I mopped those floors? Did I look at that chart right? Which drops was it that I put in Meika's eyes last, was it the neo/poly/dex or was it timol? I know it wasn't the Brenzolamide, 'cause it's white. Gotta remember those color codes for each bottle top, one's red, one's yellow, one's pink - but which is which? And just when I'm beginning to get a system going, now Murphy's got a urinary tract infection, plus worms. So, now more meds for the ever-growing chart, and that sack of worm medicine for ALL of the dogs - 'cause, "if one dog has worms, most likely they all do" Have you ever seen how much medicine is in those syringes and there are <u>six</u> syringes for each of them!!!! Here's that little red card, mam!

By the way, speaking of syringes, how come these vets make it look so easy to give shots?

Maybe it's because they have an attendant and the dog is on a table, while I am standing on my head, trying to form the little tent to poke the needle in, as Murphy is bouncing around chomping down her food and backing up, at the same time trying to get away from what she knows is coming.

Here's something else to think about... How'm I s'posed to go the gym, to the grocery store, run a few errands and get back before somebody has to go out? Soooo, guess what? More pee papers and the floor gets another mopping.... the cycle goes on!!! Really though, I'm looking forward to Meika's next visit! The good doctor has promised to begin tapering Meika off the Predisone. But, guess what they are going to want when I leave? That little red card!!! The cycle goes on!!!

Is it any wonder I'm singing "Everybody go pee-pee" and we're all dancing out the back door, as they go for their nightly stroll??

*the little red card (credit card)

Calamity Jane Mows the Grass

After running out of grandchildren to mow the grass, I bought a cute little "Forrest Gump" mower. Since I had never operated a riding mower, I cautiously followed the instructions, until I was feeling pretty confident about my newly acquired mowing skills. Since we had been blessed with so much rain and the grass (or weeds) desperately needed mowing and I had a window of opportunity, so I jumped at the chance to give "Forrest" a workout. I was feeling pretty brave at first, running the mower at full speed, until I had my first scare. While I was mowing near the highway, a rock flew out from under the mower, over the mower, out to the highway, appeared to hit a car and fell onto the highway. I watched the car until it was out of sight, fully expecting it to turn around and come charging after me.

My confidence, like a balloon that had been pricked, was beginning to deflate, but I continued to mow, still expecting to see that gray car drive up at any minute.

As I began to take on the backyard, with all the shrubs and tight spots, I found myself having to slow down, back up and make wide turns. It looked so much easier when I watched my grandson on the "Zero Turn" mower. Since I was unfamiliar with judging distance, I got myself into several "tight spots." I almost knocked myself out when I tried to mow between the pump house and a large shrub. I didn't duck my head down far enough and as I went through the space, I not only hit my head on the corner of the roof, but I turned over 3 pots of soil and ran over the bird's water pan, which stuck to the tire. When I finally recovered from my head injury and pulled the water pan off the tire, I crawled back on the mower again, my confidence shaking, as well as my legs.

Next, I tackled the area I dreaded the most; inside the fence, with some really tight spots.

I felt rather proud of myself though when I rode through the gate without a hitch and was making pretty good progress at first. I was making the turns without hitting anything and was doing fairly well with backing. I did, however, have a little trouble getting out of a corner and had to back up about 6 times to get out of it. That was the least of my problems, though. It was when I started to mow around my newly planted eucalyptus tree that I had made a little fence for, that another calamity occurred. I was looking down at my cute little fence and the mower tires as I slowly started around the tree, thinking I was judging the distance correctly when I heard a crunching sound. By the time I stopped screaming and got the mower stopped, my little fence was destroyed.

When I was almost finished mowing, I saw an area under the little magnolia tree that I had missed. I realized that I would have to deal with a limb that was hanging down, so I lifted the limb up as I slowly began moving closer to the tree. It was at that point that the limb got caught in the steering wheel and I lost control of the mower.

Since the tires were spinning up against the tree, and the limb wrapped around the steering wheel, pressing into my lap, it was hard to reach the lever to turn the blade off. When I finally remembered the clutch, everything came to a stop. Within a few minutes, the mower and I were out of the tree!

After recovering from the mowing ordeal, I decided to tackle the weed eating. I had purchased a new electric weed eater but hadn't changed the spool since I bought it. Now the spool was empty. So I took out the packet that I had purchased from Lowe's and attempted to read the instructions as to how to load the spool. First of all, the print was so small, I could hardly see the writing, then when it said to "take the new spool and push it onto the boss in the cassette" - I realized I was lost. I couldn't even understand the pictures! I was really in trouble when the instructions said to "unfasten the end of the cutting lines and guide the line into one of the eyelets!!!" That's when both lines got loose and went everywhere but into the eyelets!!

I finally got control of them, wound them back up, figured out who the boss was, snapped the thing back together and thought I was ready to start weed eating. What a racket when I turned it on. By the time I had finished weed eating the back yard, the thing had eaten up all but one little piece of line. I couldn't help but think, "this weed eater not only eats weeds, it eats the line too!!"

What a day! Maybe I need to paint my yard green or just move to the city!!

Who Needs A Man?

There are some definite disadvantages to being a woman, alone. Like when your car or your friend's car won't start. In this case it was my friend Tammy's car that wouldn't start.

We had such a nice visit, spending the weekend doing fun things, browsing at Hobby Lobby, watching movies, not having to cook. No pressure. No time limits. Stopping to eat at Hickory Tavern, even though it wasn't dinner time. Lingering a little too long over that cup of coffee and being late for church. Spending the afternoon visiting a friend, leisurely chatting and reading. Long naps, sleeping late, just being lazy – what a treat!

Then Monday morning arrives and time to return to reality. Tammy's packed and ready to leave, but her car won't start. Don't know how to attach those cables, even though I've watched "the men folks" do it plenty of times. Why didn't I pay attention? Which cable connects to what, to where? What do those colors mean? OK, Tammy's got instructions with her cables, so we'll try it, but now, we realize her car is parked between a tree and a holly bush. Besides that, both batteries are located on the left side. After carefully reading the instructions three or four times out loud, stretching those extra long cables out to reach both batteries, the cables are connected and I start my car. As Tammy gets in her car and turns the ignition, we hold our breath. Then we hear that beautiful sound. Her engine is firing up!

Who needs a man??

Big Day at the Pregnancy Center

The day was planned carefully, right down to the minute – no time to spare – church, grab a bit to eat, finish packing the car, then jump in the car and head for the pregnancy center for Open House.

We had worked so hard getting into our new facility, turning a ramshackle, dirty old mill into our shiny, newly painted facility, with three times the space we had previously. We had faced one delay after another; then, rains that almost destroyed everything we had moved, but we prevailed, burning the midnight oil to get to the big day.

That day, after picking an armload of fresh flowers from the yard, I realized I needed more vases, so I dashed out to the barn to collect a few more vases. Just as I passed a stack of folding outdoor chairs, they began crashing to the floor, with me on top of them.

As I fell, the metal arm of one of the chairs caught my right leg, just above my ankle. I immediately knew the cut was bad, but didn't realize how bad it was until I felt the rush of blood. When I finally saw the cut, it was ugly and realized, then, that my plans would change; instead of being at the pregnancy center for the big day, I would be in the Emergency Room.

With a heavy heart, I called the pregnancy center and told them my news, called my granddaughter to take the flowers to the center and left for the ER. A couple hours and thirteen stitches later, I was at the pregnancy center, sitting in a rocking chair with my aching leg propped up, thankful to finally be there.

An Almost Typical Christmas

The morning started out quietly. The only
thing I had to prepare for the family
Christmas dinner was cornbread dressing. I
thought I was organized, had everything I
needed, and then I realized I forgot to buy
chicken broth. Was it a subconscious thing,
that I just didn't want to buy it, since I don't
eat meat? Luckily, I found a package of
chicken breast in the freezer that was left by
Christina, a former housemate. It had freezer
burn on it; however, after thawing it out, it
seemed to be okay, so I put it on the stove to
cook while I started cutting up celery and
onions. After several phone calls and veggie
cutting, I decided to stop, eat breakfast and
open my gifts. As I was finishing my
breakfast, I noticed smoke, then a blaze
coming from a paper towel that I left too
close to the burner. I grabbed the paper
towel (not smart), threw it in the sink and
sprayed the fire out with the water nozzle.

I soon forgot my little scare in the kitchen as I started opening my gifts. It wasn't long, though, until the smell of smoke coming from the kitchen jogged my attention. As I ran to the kitchen I saw that smoke was quickly filling the house. As I grabbed the pot and headed out the back door with it, I realized I had left the burner on high and the chicken and my favorite pot were burned to a crisp! So now, not only do I not have any chicken broth, the chicken I was going to use for broth is sitting outside on the picnic table, smoking, I'm not finished chopping the celery and onions, the living room is strewn with gifts, wrapping paper and ribbons and I'm back to square one. Then I remembered a chicken thigh in the freezer, that I had bought for Maddie when she was sick. So, I did what any southern cook would do, start over! By 11:00 am. the dressing was in the oven, the dishwasher was running, the wrapping paper and ribbons were picked up and I sat down to recall another disaster turned into laughter, thankful I didn't burn the house down. Merry Christmas!

Hayley's Birthday Party

Hayley's birthday was coming up soon and everyone wanted to know what she wanted to do for her birthday. "One thing I <u>don't want,</u> she said, is a party." Jean, her grandmother; however, had "other plans." She loves parties and will use most any excuse to "throw a party."

Several years ago, Jean threw a "real shindig" to celebrate the wedding of William and Kate. All the women were decked out in their finest, frilly dresses. She even provided a "chariot (a beautifully decorated golf cart) and a young man dressed in a tuxedo, to drive the golf cart, who picked up the ladies upon their arrival and delivered them to the front door of Jean's house. She carried out the William and Kate theme throughout the house and yard, including napkins and trinkets with "William and Kate" on them. It was quite a party.

So, Jean went ahead with her plans for Hayley's party, in spite of Hayley's protests and invited family, friends and anyone she talked to, with her usual invitation, "Honey, we're having a party, come on over."

Hayley's birthday arrived and I went to Jean's house for the party. I walked into the kitchen area and saw a long table piled up with all sorts of delicious food and people I didn't know, sitting around eating and talking. I then walked into the dining room and found the same scenario. I saw a group of people gathered around the pool, so, since no one noticed me, I slipped out the back door. Just about the time I started to ask if anyone had seen Hayley, I saw her coming around the side of the house. When she saw me, she came over and with a look of confusion, asked me who all those strangers were inside the house. I told her I didn't know them either and asked her if it wasn't her party. She said, "Yes, but you know how Jean is, she loves a party!"

The Potential Hazards of Bread Making

It could happen to you.

You might be attempting to make your favorite whole wheat, sour dough bread recipe.

You have all the ingredients laid out.

You begin adding the first ingredients when you knock the oil off the stove.

You, then have canola oil running down the side of the stove, on the floor and since you forgot to put your apron on, you have oil splattered all over your shirt.

You, by the way, have knocked your glasses off in your attempt to catch the cup as it was flying through the air.

It was then that you notice that one of the lenses in your glasses has fallen out into the puddle of oil on the floor.

You, as all good bread makers know, must continue the process of the bread making, since the water is just the right temperature and the yeast has already been added. By this time JoJo, the cat, has discovered the puddle of oil. He tastes it, then walks through it and with his oily feet, proceeds into the living room for a nap, with every step leaving his greasy tracks on the carpet, while,

You, diligently continue on with the recipe, straining your eyes through oil soaked glasses until,

You, realize you had picked up the wrong bowl for mixing the dough and with each stir, this flimsy bowl bends and twists, as if trying to run away from the spoon.

You, then, upon finishing your "not so favorite recipe," you try to clean up the oil soaked floor.

After several moppings, you give up and cover the kitchen floor with scatter rugs.

Attempting this experiment is not advised, since: "IT HAPPENED TO ME!!"

Green Hair

Almost as soon as I heard the sound of the car drive up and the car door slam, I heard the screaming. Thinking it might be a real crisis, Kristen and I ran to see what the commotion was all about. It took a few seconds to understand what Christina was saying between the screams. Then I understood; she was pointing to her hair, which she was saying was ruined. When I told her it looked fine to me, the screams only got louder. Kristen and I tried to calm her down and make some sense of what she was trying to tell us. Finally, as her screams turned to sobs, the picture became a little clearer. A friend of Christina's, who was in the cosmetology program at the college, had volunteered to put blonde streaks in her beautiful black hair but now the streaks that were supposed to be blonde were reddish orange. All she could think about was that it was Valentine's Day and she had a big date that night. Every time we told her that her hair looked good, was very becoming or that it would grow out, the sobs turned to screams again.

As we tried to console her, I wanted to laugh but tried to hold it together until I left the room. This picture had begun to feel vaguely familiar. Before long we were all sitting on the bed doubled over in laughter as I told them the story of a similar incident in my life many years ago.

I had just applied for a new job when I got a call to come for an interview. The night before the interview, a friend talked me into letting her "frost" my hair. You'd have to know this friend to know that was my first mistake. She said, "Oh, sure, honey, I can do it." I knew I was in trouble when I saw the scissors and asked her what she was doing. She said, "it's taking too long to pull all this hair through those little tiny holes, I'm just going to cut the holes bigger." Then she began pulling my hair by the chunks, through the now enlarged holes. It was only when I washed my hair out did I see the results of not following the directions. I screamed, "it's orange, my hair is orange!!!" My friend didn't seem to think anything was wrong. She said, "Oh, honey, it looks fine." When I asked her if she couldn't put something on it to cover it up, she said, "No, it'll just have to grow out."

Then I remembered my interview the next day and panicked. I ran to the store and bought a bottle of dark brown hair color. It looked worse. I was sick. I didn't have any choice though, so I went to my interview the next day and amazingly got the job. However, from that day on, my boss never let me live down my "green hair" and told me that, under those florescent lights in my office, my hair not only glowed in the dark but in the daytime. I guess that's why everyone was so friendly when they walked down the hall, past my office.

To protect the "innocent," the name of my friend is not mentioned.

Cousin Gary's Surprise Birthday Party

One of the cousins had a brilliant idea: Let's
surprise Cousin Gary for his birthday.
We gathered from the four corners of the
county; it seemed, and headed for Ellerbe. It
was to be a potluck lunch – one person took
plates, cups, and utensils; one took
Kentucky Fried Chicken with all the
trimmings; one took drinks and ice;
somebody even brought a card.
After driving for what seemed to be an hour
or more – each turn taking us deeper into the
wilderness – we finally arrived at the old
homestead. When we three cousins arrived,
we thought it rather strange that the other
cousins were all standing outside. After
several attempts to get Cousin Gary to the
door, one of the cousins located the key and
let the other cousins in, only to find Penny,
the dog, and a couple of brown surprises that
she had left on the floor.

Soon, plans were under way for a tailgate birthday party for the absentee cousin – birthday cake included. But, as soon as Penny smelled the chicken, she arrived at the party, bringing more "surprises," right in the middle of the party. As soon as she left a surprise and a cousin cleaned it up, she came back around with another. Only when Penny was removed from the scene was the party able to continue.

One of the cousins constructed a table for the birthday cake out of a wheelbarrow, a 2×4 and a ladder. Before the cousins finished off their meal, the temperatures began to drop, and the group followed the sunshine as it began to wane, down to the driveway, savoring each beam of light. In spite of the cold, a cousin brought out ice cream. The group shivered while enjoying it, along with the birthday cake. By the time dessert was finished, the sun had almost disappeared and the group was searching the cars for coats and gloves.

As pictures were made to memorialize Cousin Gary's birthday, we noticed the odd assortment of coats, hats and gloves that had been gathered.

One cousin (a man) had on a ladies coat; a child had on a man's coat; one had on a "safari looking" hat; and I had a glove and a sock on my hands.

We did change Cousin Gary's card before we headed back to our four corners. It said, "Sorry you missed your party – wish you were here!"

Night of the Frogs

The evening started out uneventful. It was
around 6:00 pm. I had finished dinner and
was cleaning up the kitchen, getting ready to
sit down and watch a little TV, when, out of
the corner of my eye I noticed something
moving on the floor, near the backdoor. As I
got closer to the little black spot, about the
size of my thumbnail, it started jumping
toward me. I realized, then, that it was a
baby frog. I remembered, that morning, as I
sat on the back porch eating my breakfast, I
had seen about a dozen of the same little
frogs hopping around the patio. At the time,
I thought they were cute, but that night when
my nightmare began, they were not cute at
all.

At first there was one, then two, then more
than I could count. I grabbed a paper towel
and began picking them up, running to the
front door and throwing them out. I tried to
keep a cool head but inwardly I was freaking
out.

All I could think of was the plague of frogs in the Bible and imagined them jumping in my bed that night. I realized they were coming in under the back door so I tried packing a towel under the door but they kept coming! I later found out they were coming in over the top of the weather stripping on the door. I looked out through the panes in the door and saw them hopping all around the back porch. When I had collected all the frogs in the house and secured their entrance, it was 11:00 pm and I realized I had been chasing frogs for about 5 hours. I was exhausted, so I took a hot bath, and went to bed, trying to relax but every time I closed my eyes I was still imagining there were frogs still in the house and where they might be – maybe in my bed!? I got up several times searching for frogs that might have escaped.

The first thing I did the next morning was to check the house and the back porch for frogs. The few that I found on the porch and patio I collected and put in an old pitcher with a little water and a rock for them to sit on with the plan to give them to my great grandson for his critter collection.

When I told his grandmother about my plan, she discouraged it, so I took them down to the lake and watched the seven little frogs happily hopping down to the water.

The interesting thing about "The Night of the Frogs;" the frogs were there for just that one night. Even the neighbors that had seen frogs that night said they only saw them that one night (but none of them had the experience that I did.)

I'm just glad they are gone and that nightmare is over!

A Pool in the Kitchen

I have a pool in my kitchen. It's not very big and not too deep, but it's there, all the same – this gaping hole, with mounds of dirt and concrete piled up on each side, and pipes, just staring at me. Thankfully, there's no water in the pool now that the problem had been found.

It all started on Sunday morning when I noticed a little puddle of water at the edge of the dishwasher. As I cleaned up that puddle I noticed another little puddle beginning to form in front of the sink. After attempting to clean up more puddles, I realized my efforts were futile and ran to the pump house to turn the water off.

You don't realize how much you depend on water until you turn that facet on and there's nothing there. So by the time the plumber arrived early Monday morning, he was a welcome sight.

I soon found out that I had bigger problems than a couple of little puddles on the kitchen floor. The search began. Counters had to be cleared off, cabinets cleaned out, washer, dryer and refrigerator pulled out from the wall, and now, a hole in the bathroom wall, ladders to get into the attic to look at the pipes there (the first ladder was too short), several trips to the Burney Hardware, a trip to Richmond Reynolds – the whole house turned upside down. Water, mud, and dirty towels, that I can't hang outside because of the rain and can't wash them because the water is turned off. Searching, searching for the elusive pipe coming up out of the ground, which connects all the other pipes. Decisions, questions. Finally after deciding to start digging under the sink; because my house is built on a concrete slab; using a machine similar to a jackhammer (with a shorter handle), the tedious drilling through concrete began. After what seemed like an eternity of earth shattering noise, and mounds of dirt that had to dug out, the suspect was found. The rather small hole in the pipe, when the water was turned back on, produced enough water to form a pool in a matter of minutes.

After eight hours of work, the pipe was repaired, the water in the pool had evaporated, but the gaping hole and the mounds of wet dirt under my sink in the kitchen, remain, for now, and I attempt to put the house back in partial order while the fan is drying out the dirt.

The moral of this story is: don't put pipes in the ground and pour the house's foundation on top of it!

A Bum Comes to Church

I had gone with a group of friends to Atlanta for a conference. We were having a wonderful time, going to meetings during the day, coming back to our friends' motor home, having dinner and going back to the evening meetings.

One afternoon, someone suggested we visit the slums, where the homeless lived. We met a man, shared the gospel with him, prayed for him and invited him to have dinner with us. As I sat across from him in the little motor home, his body odor was so strong and nauseating, it almost made me sick. He spoke very little but devoured his food and when spoken to he kept repeating "just trying to make it, just trying to make it."

That night, he agreed to go to the conference with us, as our honored guest. Before long, we noticed him fidgeting and excused himself to go the restroom. We searched for the poor old man we found in the slums but never found him.

The Pinehurst Hawk

There have been several sightings of a hawk
around the Pinehurst area for several years.
The first time that I knew of this hawk was
in 2013. I was a patient in Moore Regional
Hospital on the lower floor of the cancer
wing, after having surgery. As I recall, it
was late at night and my daughters was
staying with me. I was rather groggy from
pain medicine but awoke suddenly to my
daughters' screaming that there was a hawk
in the window. I was fascinated by the sight
of the hawk but my daughters were freaking
out, thinking it was some kind of an omen. I
think their screams scared the poor creature
away.

Not long after that I saw a picture of the
hawk in the local newspaper and a story of
other sightings of a hawk in the vicinity of
the hospital.

Then, a few days before he had surgery, my son spotted a hawk in his backyard in Pinehurst with a snake at it's feet, then picking the snake up and carrying it away.

Could this be the same hawk? Could this be my family's "guardian hawk?"

Building A House

While trying to rest and recuperate
from my ordeal with Pasteurella,
an infection I developed from a
cat scratch, I spent a number of
days at Jeff's house (Jeff is one of
my two sons). From my little
room at Jeff's house, I could see
and hear a huge, neighboring
house being repaired from termite
damage. As I would lie there
listening, it seemed there were
hundreds of hammers and all sorts
of tools working throughout the
day. It was rather comforting,
hearing the workers out there
REBUILDING that beautiful old
home that termites had tried to
destroy.

Later, as I lay there inside the
"tunnel" of an MRI machine, with
earplugs in my ears, I listened to
all the hammering and banging
(sounds from the machine) going
on.

Those machine sounds, that seemed to surround me on every side, reminded me of being at Jeff's house. I began to imagine the MRI noises as coming from different types of tools that would build a house; I compared the sounds to those I heard at Jeff's house. I tried to picture all the tools I seemed to be hearing, remembering the jack hammer, as being the most prevalent. I could even "see" the roof, with its high peaks and wondered what sort of jack hammer could be used on a roof! I began to imagine the work going on in each room, designing each room in my mind, not only the inside and outside of each room, but the roof as well. I continued to "work" on my imaginary house, watching every little fine detail, down to "seeing" the grass, the flowers – even the "For Sale" sign in the front yard, until its completion, just prior to exiting the second MRI machine.

Toward the completion of my "imaginary house," I began thinking about my body, the temple of the Holy Spirit. As with the "imaginary house,"my house, my "temple" had been attacked by the enemy, who was trying again to destroy it. I thought of how God is using different tools to restore my body, knowing that God <u>will</u> complete the good work He began in me. My spiritual house isn't complete yet, as God is still working on <u>this</u> house, but I praise Him, that even in the "tunnel" of that MRI machine, He was there, speaking to me, even giving me another story to write. As the old song goes, "God's still working on me".

Every house is built and furnished by someone but the Builder of all things and Finisher (of the entire equipment of all things) is God. Hebrews 3:4 (Amplified)

Made in the USA
Columbia, SC
09 June 2020